GAME OF MY LIFE

NEW YORK

GIANTS

GAME OF MY LIFE

NEW YORK

GIANTS

MEMORABLE STORIES OF GIANTS FOOTBALL

KEN PALMER
FOREWORD BY TIKI BARBER

SPORTS
PUBLISHING

Sports Publishing books may be purchased in bulk at special discounts for sales
promotion, corporate gifts, fund-raising, or educational purposes. Special editions can
also be created to specifications. For details, contact the Special Sales Department,
Sports Publishing, 307 West 36th Street, 11th Floor, New York, NY 10018 or
sportspubbooks@skyhorsepublishing.com.

Sports Publishing® is a registered trademark of Skyhorse Publishing, Inc.®,
a Delaware corporation.

Visit our website at www.sportspubbooks.com

10 9 8 7 6 5 4 3 2 1

Library of Congress Cataloging-in-Publication Data is available on file.

ISBN: 978-1-61321-243-1

Printed in the United States of America

THIS BOOK IS DEDICATED TO THE MEMORY OF
MY LOVING FATHER, RICHARD PALMER,
AND MY BEST FRIEND, STEPHEN BRAYNOCK.
TWO BETTER, MORE CARING, HONEST AND GENEROUS
MEN THE WORLD WILL NEVER SEE.

CONTENTS

FOREWORD

American society loves sports—the figures, the stories, the dramas of competition. There is a sense of ownership over one's favorite team or idolized player. This is true for all genres of athletic competition, but the game that exemplifies it most is football and, more specifically, America's most popular stage, the NFL. In particular, New York has a strong connection with its athletes. One of the reasons that I loved playing my whole career in New York was that I knew those who watched understood what they were watching and could appreciate the successes and dissect the failures.

A necessary part of the sports arena is the sports journalist, whose job it is to report those triumphs and defeats, to reflect and opine, and to paint the picture for posterity.

They help us to understand that the games go beyond the Xs and Os, and that the stories within the stories are often what make them memorable.

For many, football is passion, not only for those inside the huddle, but countless others outside the lines; they are cheering and booing; they observe the struggle and relish in the majesty. Their talking point is often only the bottom line—the "W" or the "L."

But sometimes, if you follow close enough, you'll come across the back story, that writers like Kenny P capture and present in the athletes' eyes . . . and all of a sudden the games have a whole new meaning.

Enjoy!

Tiki

ACKNOWLEDGMENTS

I'd like to extend my sincerest thanks to several members of the Giants organization whose help was essential in writing this book. Special thanks go out to John Mara, Ernie Accorsi, and the public relations staff, especially Peter John-Baptiste, Avis Roper, and Phyllis Hayes. And most importantly a big thank you goes out to all the former and current players who were so generous with their time.

GAME OF MY LIFE

NEW YORK

GIANTS

Chapter 1

TIKI BARBER

THE YOUNG LIFE OF TIKI BARBER

Tiki Barber will be the first to admit that he wouldn't be where he is today without his loving mother and brother. Geraldine Barber was forced to raise her two boys on her own when her husband, James, who played football at Virginia Tech, left before the Barber twins, Tiki and Ronde, were even old enough to remember.

"It was busy for my mom growing up," Tiki explained. "She was a single mom raising us, so she worked a couple jobs to make ends meet and give us the things that we needed."

Tiki and his fellow Pro Bowl brother Ronde, a cornerback for the Buccaneers, never were deprived of anything despite their single-parent childhood.

"It was good because we had each other and there was always love in our household," Tiki said. "We never wanted for anything, which is a testament to how hard she worked.

"I think those ideals and work ethics are what stick with my brother and I today and make us as successful as we've become. She's been great and supportive in everything we've done. She never pushed us, just encouraged us. It's a testament to her how we turned out."

Born in Montgomery County Hospital in Blacksburg, Virginia, the Barber boys grew up in Roanoke, Virginia, as close as two brothers can be. After superb high school careers at Cave Spring High, it was obvious that the two-sport stars were heading to the same college.

"We were heavily recruited because we were stars in both football and track and field," Tiki said. "Michigan was up there and Clemson and we even thought about going to the West Coast. But we were only 170 pounds at graduation. It wasn't like we were some stud football players that were certain to succeed. We wanted to go somewhere that we'd get the fullest experience as a student-athlete. The University of Virginia was that place."

Growing up, Tiki and Ronde were inseparable. Wherever one went, the other was certain to follow.

"It wasn't until we were seniors in high school and I went to Busch Gardens with my girlfriend, that was the first time my brother and I slept apart from each other," Tiki said. "We were roommates in college so I always had someone there to encourage and lift me up and give me direction."

Tiki Barber has been pointed in the right direction ever since.

THE GAME OF MY LIFE
GIANTS VS. REDSKINS—OCTOBER 30, 2005
BY TIKI BARBER

This game was especially meaningful because our beloved owner, Wellington Mara, passed away earlier in the week. From my perspective, that week was almost as if it was written as a story.

We beat Denver the previous Sunday, which was the last game Wellington saw. He passed away that Tuesday. But because we won against Denver, we had Monday off. Coach (Tom) Coughlin never gives us days off, but he did, which turned out to be a blessing because I had an opportunity at the behest of the Mara family to go up and see Mr. Mara and sit with him for a few hours. Jeremy Shockey was there when I arrived and then he left. I got to say prayers with him and thank him for everything he'd done for me and my career. That meant a lot to me.

I was the last player to see him alive. He passed away that next morning.

That entire week was solemn. It was hard. We were used to seeing him there and suddenly this presence that had been a part of New York Giants history forever was not there anymore, and you could feel it.

Tiki Barber holds virtually every Giants rushing record.
Anthony J Causi, Icon Images

The funeral was on Friday. It was tough. John Mara's eulogy was perfect. It captured the essence of Wellington better than any historian could have told it. He wrote it and delivered it beautifully.

When we came out of the funeral mass, there were thousands of Giants fans there, across the street from St. Patrick's. It was amazing and inspiring despite the tragedy.

Then we headed back to the stadium for practice. It was an overcast day, but right when we got out there, there was this one beam of sunlight that came down on our practice field and only lasted like 10 minutes. I turned to coach Tom Coughlin and said, "That's Wellington looking down on us." He said, "I think you're right."

You can't make it up, the things that happened surrounding this week and this game.

Wellington was old school with everything that he did, including his philosophies on winning football games and running the ball. That game was nothing but me, my offensive line, and our game plan to run it straight down the throats of the Redskins, one of our most heated rivals.

That morning was the same for me. There was nothing different as far as preparation. But you knew you wanted to have the right day. For whatever reason, I had my best day, at least in my mind, and that means a lot to me.

The first play of the game was a 57-yard run. I just took the ball and took off. It was almost as if every play the holes were gaping. After the first play, I knew it was going to be a big day. One play in and I knew this was something special. It turned out to be just that.

We were all in a zone, playing with a higher purpose and a higher sense of meaning. I had another long run (59 yards) and came to the sideline, and Timmy McDonnell, who's been one of my closest friends since I've been here, jokingly asked if I was going to keep teasing him and getting caught or actually finally score one for him.

Timmy is one of Wellington's 40 grandchildren and was my ball boy from the time I got here. Right then and there, I told him I was going to score one for him.

Late in the third quarter, I ran a four-yard draw and jumped into the end zone. I dropped the ball after scoring and then immediately picked it up, ran directly to the sideline and gave it to Timmy. I said, "Timmy, this is for you and your family. I love you, I love your grandfather, and I can't thank you enough for what you guys have always meant to me."

Then I took myself out of the game. I had broken my single-game rushing record that day, and was only 12 yards short of the Giants single-game rushing record. I easily could have gotten it. To tell you the truth, I could have rushed for 300 yards that game.

When I scored that touchdown for Timmy, it was as if I had fulfilled that day. That's all that mattered to me. It was about me individually accomplishing something. It was about showing my gratitude and my desire to give back to the Mara family. This was the only way I could do it—have a day like this during the game we honored Wellington.

I think about it and wonder why I was able to have such a big day. Why was I able to say goodbye? I don't have an answer for it, but I'm fortunate. It's an experience I will never forget.

After the game, we just went out to eat at Primola on the Upper East Side and reflected on it. It's one of those things that didn't make sense why it happened, but I'm glad it did.

We played with a higher meaning, myself included. The guys up front were great. They didn't have the relationship I had with the Mara family, but they knew what was at stake.

There's no question that I've had bigger statistical games. Against Philadelphia to go to the playoffs in 2002, I had 276 all-purpose yards. Against the Chiefs in 2005, I set a Giants record with 220 rushing yards. But for what this meant to this organization and the Mara family, there was no bigger game. For me to have that kind of game on that day was special and I'm thankful for it.

A lot of it was a blur. I really only remember three plays—the two long runs and the touchdown for Timmy. But it was just one of those days.

It's the most special win I've ever been a part of and the most special day I've ever had.

GAME RESULTS

This wasn't just any ordinary 57-yard run. It was almost as if divine intervention played a role as Tiki Barber took the handoff on the game's opening play, burst through the line and took off, sparking his entire club in what would be a 36-0 blowout of the Redskins on the day the club honored its beloved owner.

"I don't recall a lot about the game because I was still numb," Giants President/CEO John Mara said. "I certainly remember after the game seeing him (Barber) in the locker room and hugging him. I do remember that he had a big game that day. He's been a special player for his whole career, both on and off the field.

"My father thought very highly of him. It was fitting that he had such a big game that day because he's been such a great representative for us. Certainly none of us were surprised by his performance. We probably should have expected it."

After another lengthy run and a short TD, Barber's afternoon was complete. He finished with 206 yards on only 24 carries, a whopping 8.6 yards per tote.

"It was a very emotional week for him," Barber's wife Ginny told *The Giant Insider*. "To play like this was just a good tribute to Mr. Mara."

At the time, Barber's 206 yards were the second highest ever in Giants history. Gene "Choo Choo" Roberts held the record with 218 yards against the Chicago Cardinals on November 12, 1950. Barber's previous high was 203 yards against Philadelphia on December 28, 2002. Barber went on in 2005 to post a 220-yard contest against Kansas City to set the all-time mark, which he then broke in his final regular-season game against the Washington Redksins' in 2006 with a 234-yard, three-touchdown performance.

"I don't think he set out to break any records, but he just wanted Mr. Mara to be proud of him and the team," Ginny Barber said.

Everyone was proud of Barber, including his coach.

"It was outstanding," Tom Coughlin said to *The Giant Insider*. "Tiki had an outstanding game and the run game was outstanding."

Timmy McDonnell is one of the late Wellington Mara's 40 grandkids, and definitely the one closest to Barber. McDonnell started working as a ball boy at Giants training camp when he was nine years old. He was especially excited about his buddy's accomplishments.

"Tiki's game against the Redskins made all of us proud," McDonnell said. "I think that for our family it was very fitting Tiki had the kind of day he did against the Redskins. He was without question one of my grandfather's favorites. He has always represented the Giants with class and dignity and always made my grandfather proud on and off the field. His play along with the rest of the team was inspiring. It was Giants football—running the football and playing great defense against our division rival—football Pop Pop was proud of."

The most emotional moment of the game came when Barber scored a four-yard TD late in the third quarter and gave McDonnell the ball.

"Tiki and I have always been close," McDonnell stated. "I still don't know if I can put into words what getting the ball meant. I had so many emotions through the day, that when he flipped me the ball and hugged me I didn't know how to react, whether to smile or cry. I will always remember that moment and always be grateful to Tiki. The ball is in a case with the ticket from the game and sits in my office."

John Mara was especially impressed with Barber's overall performance—and not just during that game.

"It meant a lot to my family to know that Tiki thought enough of my father to come out there and spend some time with him during those last couple days," Mara recalled. "It's not an easy thing to sit through, somebody dying. It showed a lot of character on his part."

As did his superb performance against Washington.

Chapter 2

OTTIS ANDERSON

THE YOUNG LIFE OF OTTIS ANDERSON

Ottis Anderson drew his marvelous running skills from quite an unlikely source.

"My habits and running style went all the way back to chasing rabbits as a kid," said Anderson, who grew up in Florida. "Rabbits have quick bursts of speed, but if you stayed behind them long enough you could catch them."

For much of his youth, Anderson also spent time trying to catch his older brother, Marvin, who tragically died when Ottis was in sixth grade.

"My brother was probably one of the best players that ever played football, but he died in college," Anderson said. "He would have been as good as Gale Sayers, Mike Garrett, and guys like that. From what I was told from different players that knew him, as good as I was, I couldn't have carried his jockstrap."

Just one mention of his mentor—in life and in football—puts an immediate smile on Anderson's face.

"He was older," he continued, "Marvin 'Smoke' Anderson. They used to say, 'Where there's smoke, there's fire.' They used to call me 'Little Smoke' for a long time."

Anderson learned how to be the man of the house from Marvin's example.

"My brother had a dream that he wanted to move my Mom and us out of the projects and give us a better chance at life," he said. "He knew through athletics he could accomplish that. He died with that dream of making it happen. When he died I instantly became him."

That meant making sure to always care for and obey his mother.

"My dad wasn't much in my life," Anderson explained. "My mom was the one that taught me all about being a man and being disciplined. She used to tell me, 'Son, I work too hard; don't embarrass me.' I knew I couldn't go home and embarrass her; I didn't want to embarrass her."

After starring at Forest Hill High School in West Palm Beach, Anderson received a full ride to the University of Miami, where he met one of the men most responsible for his success.

"At UM, Lou Saban came in as coach my junior year," he said. "He saw my potential and told me that, if I did what he said and worked hard enough, he could almost assure that I'd be one of the best professional athletes that ever played the game. He really had a lot to do with honing in my skills."

THE GAME OF MY LIFE
GIANTS VS. BILLS—SUPER BOWL XXV,
JANUARY 27, 1991
BY OTTIS ANDERSON

If you look at all the Giants games in my career, this is by far the most significant and memorable. You have millions of people watching. It was important to me because of what it represented at that time, the impact the Gulf War had on it, and the magnitude of how many people watched that particular game. Winning Super Bowl MVP honors is as good as it gets.

We had a team meeting the morning of the game, and then we broke off into individual meetings. One of the comments I made in that meeting was that I was going to win Most Valuable Player. Lewis Tillman kind of laughed and said, "How do you figure you're going to win Most Valuable Player?' I said, "Well, someone has to win it, and why not me?" We kind of laughed about that.

But that goes back to my playing days at the University of Miami. I mentioned to my roommate Kenny Johnson that, if I ever played a Super

Ottis Anderson carries the ball against Buffalo during Super Bowl XXV in Tampa, Florida.
Rich Pilling, Icon Images

Bowl in the state of Florida and was the featured running back, I'd win Most Valuable Player. Twelve years later it did come true.

A friend of mine, Brandon Steiner, called the morning of the game and told me that I was going to be MVP. The phone in my room was blocked so it was surprising that he even got through.

The night before the game, a handful of us—including Dave Duerson, Stacy Robinson, and William Roberts—we were up playing cards all night. The coaches came by to run us to bed, but we just got right back up. We probably stayed up until six in the morning. We didn't want to sleep. It was the biggest game of our lives. One way of holding off the butterflies and all the anticipation was keeping that night from ending. Like kids on Christmas Eve, we stayed up so late that we were able to sleep most of the day—and then we were ready.

But when you look at that game you have to look at what was going on in the world at the time: the Gulf War. Many of the players used to go to the stadium early, but they wouldn't even let the players in early. They wouldn't let anyone in until the busses arrived. Roy Green, who's a very close friend from my days with the Cardinals, was walking, and Bill Parcells picked him up and took him on the bus with us. Otherwise, he would have never gotten in.

This is a game that they talked about not even playing, but it was very important and good for the country and the league to play it. When Whitney Houston stood there and sang "The National Anthem," it was very, very emotional for all of us.

We felt like we were underdogs when we arrived. But that was reminiscent of when we played the 49ers (in the NFC Championship game). I told Mark Ingram on the sideline before Matt Bahr hit the game-winning field goal for us in San Fran, "We are going to Tampa because this is my destiny."

The 49ers had already sent all of their equipment to Tampa. When we showed up at the hotel, we were told that it was reserved for the 49ers. Bill (Parcells) said, "Well, they ain't coming."

We just had fun; we were underdogs. Everyone from the people of Tampa to the Bills thought that the 49ers should have been there instead, and they took us lightly. They didn't think we could win it. They said with a backup quarterback and an old running back that should be out of the league that there was no way we could win it. But you can't measure heart, determination, and perseverance. The Bills talked all game long about the fact that we shouldn't be there, that we had too many old players on our team. They kept saying it was their destiny, their time.

That all changed when we ran off that tremendously long drive to start the third quarter, which was capped by my touchdown. I knew we were going to run a straight-ahead dive play and try to utilize my size. Hopefully, I could go over the top, but I always had a fear of jumping over the top. I always thought I was too old and too big to try to dive over the top. I didn't have the vertical I had when I came out of the University of Miami. So I knew I wasn't going airborne. It just so happened that the play allowed me to bounce outside where I was able to go in standing up.

When I crossed into the end zone, I was going to spike the ball, but then I thought, "This is a Super Bowl ball." So I flipped it to the ref and he flipped it back to me. I ran to the sideline, and I knew the guys were going to jump on me and tackle me because it was such an exciting moment for everybody. But I ran away from them because I knew they were going to tackle me and pile up on me. You don't ever want to be on the bottom of the pile because you can't breathe, and they're always slow in piling off.

A few other plays stand out for me from that game, like my big run to the sideline late in the third quarter, where I gave the big uppercut forearm to Mark Kelso. That was big. A few plays prior to that, I ran a cutback right up the middle, and Kelso came up to hit me. I got lower than him and really ripped through him. I could hear him grunting. At that point in time, I think I took a little steam out of him. When I hit him, I didn't slow down, so I knew I had won that battle. So a couple plays later, when I turned the corner and saw him, what I wanted to do was make him think about how to hit me—whether he wanted to come up and try to push me out of bounds or go low on me. But as I started bringing my arm down low I saw his head kind of duck and focus on my arm and what I was going to do to him. When he got close enough to me, I knew that if I could rip his head from low to high I could take his helmet and him backward and just rip through his tackle attempt. If it weren't for Cornelius Bennett trailing in the background I might have scored a second touchdown. Kelso did not tackle me. I was going through his attempt, but Cornelius tackled me from behind. Kelso didn't want any part of me.

I also remember one of the best blocks I had all year, against a blitzing Cornelius Bennett. I came across the formation and just stoned him and took him to the ground. Shane Conlan can also tell you that one of the first plays out of the box, I was blocking him and broke his facemask and almost knocked him out. I jammed my neck and darn near knocked myself out.

Needless to say, waiting and watching as Scott Norwood's kick sailed wide right was dramatic. And then the emotion of knowing you had won the Super Bowl immediately washed over you.

The night before the game, Disney representatives came to a bunch of the players that they thought could be MVPs. We had a choice whether to say we wanted to dedicate the win to our troops or say that we were going to Disney. I said I wanted to dedicate it to the troops. People from Disney were on the sidelines and told me that if Norwood missed the field goal that I'd be the MVP. But people on Buffalo's sideline were telling Thurman (Thomas) that if the kick was good, he'd be the Most Valuable Player. But even after he missed I just thought I was the Disney MVP, not necessarily the game MVP.

Ironically, the first person who told me I had won the honor was Lewis Tillman. He came up all excited saying, "You said it, you said it, you said it," and then he told me I was the MVP. All I could say was, "Wow." Bill called me up on the dais with George Young and the commissioner. But there was so much celebration, I don't think it totally hit me until I got back to my locker and sat down and thought about it.

One funny recollection I have from the postgame locker room was when Bill Parcells said, "Winning the Super Bowl is better than having sex." I told Parcells, "Then you ain't having good sex. Because there's nothing better than good sex."

I know that winning that trophy meant that I was the one recognized, but all of us knew that it was a total team effort. But the award put me into a very elite group of players that I never expected to join—like Bart Starr and Roger Staubach. Until someone else comes along for the Giants, Phil Simms and I will always be the only Super Bowl MVPs in Giants history.

I just believe that that Super Bowl was for not only the Giants but also me individually for what I predicted years before that.

GAME RESULTS

A back-and-forth contest that came down to the final gun turned on one single possession. New York's 14-play, 75-yard drive that used 9:29 of the third-quarter clock ended in Anderson's one-yard TD run, giving the Giants a 17-12 advantage en route to their thrilling 20-19 victory in Super Bowl XXV. New York knew that the best way to contain the explosive Bills offense, which had scored 95 combined points in its previous two playoff games, was to keep Jim Kelly and Co. off the field.

"They call us predictable and conservative, but I know one thing: I've coached this game a long time and power running wins football games," head coach Bill Parcells told *The New York Times*. "It's not always the fanciest way, but it can win games."

Anderson's ground attack helped limit the Bills to one play (Kelly taking a knee to end the first half) in a span of 13 minutes, 26 seconds from the second quarter into the third. In a dominating second-half performance, Anderson rumbled for 63 yards on 14 carries after the intermission.

"He was supposed to be washed up when he first came over here before the first Super Bowl," center Bart Oates told *The New York Times*. "Every year people have been wondering if he's going to retire, but he keeps coming back. Another five or six years and he might retire then."

"They said Ottis couldn't run on grass, and he did it two weeks in a row (NFC Championship Game at San Francisco also)," cornerback Everson Walls told *The Star-Ledger*. "O.J. can do it all."

Even members of the ferocious Bills defense knew why they came up short.

"You think you have him wrapped up and he slips through," Bills linebacker Darryl Talley told *The Star-Ledger*. "He still has the moves he had years ago. He was the difference. If we had stopped him, we would have won. No doubt about it."

But while everyone will remember Anderson's 102-yard, one-TD performance that garnered him MVP honors, Anderson said he'd never forget the contributions of backup QB Jeff Hostetler, who was filling in for the injured Phil Simms. Hostetler was battered and bruised all game long yet completed 20-of-32 passes for 222 yards and a TD.

"You have to look at the way that Hostetler took hit after hit after hit and kept coming up with a play," Anderson recalled. "A lot of people didn't realize it but there were a few series that Hostetler was on the sideline and he was totally out. I was sitting there watching them put three or four ammonium packs under his nose and there was no response. You want to talk about a warrior playing a game."

But in the end, the MVP trophy went to a warrior veteran running back.

"I feel like I'm 24, 25 years old, not 33," Anderson told *The Star-Ledger*. "But I am tired. I feel like a guy who has carried the ball 21 times for 100 yards."

Looking back on the all-time classic more than a decade and a half later, Anderson was still adamant that New York's title thriller was the all-time best Super Bowl.

"I think that will always be the best Super Bowl ever," he said. "In some of the other late, close games—St. Louis and Tennessee and New England and the Rams—had the trailing team scored at the end of the game, the game would have just gone to overtime. We were the only game that was do-or-die—that was going to be decided right then and there. Really, the whole game was played like it was do-or-die. It was like a great heavyweight championship fight. We took their best blows and they took ours. But at the end we had the last knockout punch that gave us a chance to win."

Chapter 3

HARRY CARSON

THE YOUNG LIFE OF HARRY CARSON

Growing up one of six brothers and sisters, Harry Carson described Florence, South Carolina, simply as "home."

"I was in my little neighborhood and that was all I ever knew," Carson said. "You'd go out in the morning and be out all day and no one had to worry about you. You'd play 'Cowboys and Indians' and you had a stick and that was your gun."

It wasn't long until Carson was firing shots on the football field at McClenaghan High School, where he starred in multiple sports. But, according to Carson, he could've never made the leap to South Carolina State and then the NFL without the loving guidance of his family—not to mention one very special coach—along the way.

"My family influenced me tremendously and supported me because no one else in my family played football," he explained. "When I wanted to play they supported me in that regard, whether it be in high school or college."

But it was in college that Carson and his coach, Willie Jeffries, formed the closest of bonds.

"Willie Jeffries was my mentor, so to speak," Carson said. "I learned a lot from him, and not just as a football player but as a man. He was the one that kind of led the transition from boyhood to manhood."

Jeffries, who's been on hand for Carson basically every step of the way since they met, recalls a young Carson with admiration.

"It's easy when your best player is your best person," Jeffries said. "That's just so great for a college coach, when your best player does everything right, was an honor student. He was just that kind of guy, never a problem, just a coach's dream: A player with his ability never giving you a problem of any kind, academically or socially, or anything."

During this time, Jeffries taught Carson much more than blitzes and pass coverage.

"I know everything; I mean I was like Harry's dad," Jeffries said. "I got closer to Harry as time expired, when he started playing for me and I had to start doing fatherly things or advising him to help him mature."

Carson credits his collegiate years for establishing the strong leadership ability he still possesses today.

"South Carolina State is where I learned most of my leadership skills," he said. "Anyone can follow, but as a leader you have to be willing to take chances and put your neck out on the line and deal with whatever consequences you have to deal with if you're wrong. I've always prided myself on being a team player. It's always about team and not about the individual. That's what football is, a total team sport."

THE GAME OF MY LIFE
GIANTS VS. PACKERS—SEPTEMBER 20, 1982
BY HARRY CARSON

The game in 1982 against Green Bay, right before we went on strike, personally, I think was my best game. From a statistical standpoint, I made 25 tackles in that game. And I think it was because we were all going on strike as a league after that game. I didn't have any kind of indication when we would be coming back. I remember thinking to myself, "Hell, I might as well let it all out."

The mere fact that it was the last game before the strike put me in a different mind-set. I thought that if I got hurt, then I just got hurt and it's no big deal. I'd have the whole off-season to get healthy.

Hall of Fame linebacker Harry Carson was named the NFL's top inside linebacker of all time by *Pro Football Weekly*.
George Gojkovich, Getty Images

I had 20 individual tackles and five assists. I just knew I was all over the field. When the ball was snapped, I tried to get in on every tackle that I could get in on.

I wasn't even thinking about my stats as the game went along. I was more wrapped up in the game at the time and what it was all about—playing the Green Bay Packers and the fact that it was the last game. Looking back, you can think of all sorts of different things. But as you're going through it, you're wondering what the owners were thinking and if they were actually going to pull the plug on the season. You wonder if the players were doing the right thing by going out on strike.

It was a Monday, and I hated Monday night games. It threw your whole rhythm off. Everybody else in the league had already played and we were the last game. All the guys around the league had already cleaned out their lockers and everything and we still had to go out there and play. My last thought was that we were the last and final game for however long and it was on national television.

Every time someone touched the ball, I made sure I was there. No specific tackles from that game really stand out to me, but I was obviously all over the place.

One funny thing happened during that game though. James Lofton was a Packers wide receiver and they threw a little pass across the middle to him and I tackled him. We were both on the bottom of a pile of guys. When we were down at the bottom he said, "Hey, Harry, how are you doing?" I said, "Fine, James, how are you doing?" He said, "I'm doing good." So I asked him how Beverly, his wife, was doing. He said, "She's doing good." That's definitely something that stands out about that game. In the middle of such a rugged and rough game where we're both going all out, I got to have a nice exchange with a friend of mine.

I remember during the course of the game that the lights went off and there was a delay. It was a sign and a symbol of what was going on at that time, with guys going on strike and all that.

For me, that game was just all about having fun, even though we lost. I wanted to make certain that I had fun because I didn't know when I was going to be able to play again. I remember making a couple of early stops and then going from there. You came off the field after that game thinking, "What am I going to do with my time?" None of us had any idea how long we'd be out for.

I have to admit, I've never been one of those guys who goes back and reflects on what I did personally during specific games. I more like to recall how the team did overall. I've always been that way. But I do know that I played a heck of a game that night against the Packers.

GAME RESULTS

The first *Monday Night Football* game ever played in Giants Stadium will always be remembered for everything but the final result. For the record, the Giants blew a 19-7 third-quarter lead in dropping a 27-19 decision to Green Bay.

As Carson noted, this historic game was played despite the NFL Players Association announcing a strike earlier in the day—not to mention the two separate stadium blackouts that led to 24 minutes of delay time.

But the most memorable aspect of New York's first Monday Nighter had to be Carson's remarkable 25-tackle, one-sack performance. Practically every time a Packers player was tackled, it was Carson who drove him to the ground.

After starting the '82 campaign with a loss to Atlanta, the Giants seemed in the clear to get their first win with less than two minutes remaining in the third quarter and a 12-point cushion. But that's when Carson's buddy, James Lofton, turned the momentum fully in Green Bay's favor. Lofton took a reverse handoff around the corner and raced 83 yards for a touchdown.

Giants quarterback Scott Brunner threw a pair of fourth-quarter interceptions to stall New York's comeback hopes, and the Giants dropped their second straight contest in Ray Perkins' final season at the helm.

After the game, reality struck that there would be no more football for the foreseeable future.

"When the players left the field after it was over, the fans were derisively chanting, 'Strike, Strike,'" Giants President/CEO John Mara recalled.

"Suddenly, your routine is broken up and you're in that uncomfortable situation of not knowing what the future held for you," Carson added. "That feeling was the worst."

All told, the strike lasted slightly more than two months and cost each club seven games. New York finished its abbreviated schedule with a 4-5 mark while Carson's 25-tackle outburst propelled him onto a 107-tackle season, quite impressive considering it was accomplished in only nine contests.

"I would say that Harry's performance that night was certainly indicative of how he played," Mara said. "It did not matter whether we had a good team or bad—Harry always performed like a Hall of Famer."

Chapter 4

SEAN LANDETA

THE YOUNG LIFE OF SEAN LANDETA

Sean Landeta was just like any other young boy in Baltimore in the early '70s. His choice of hero to emulate was simple: Jim O'Brien, who kicked the game-winning 32-yard field goal with five seconds to play as Baltimore's beloved Colts knocked off Dallas to win Super Bowl V, 16-13.

"Me and every other kid in Baltimore wanted to be like him," Landeta recalled, "so we went out and made that divot in the ground to put the ball in. Then we'd kick the ball over a volleyball net and pretend we won the Super Bowl."

Little did the nine-year-old Landeta know that later in life his trusty right leg would help his club, the Giants, capture a pair of NFL titles. Actually, the multisport star also considered a baseball career and almost didn't even play football at Loch Raven High School in Baltimore.

"I didn't play football until I was a senior in high school," he said. "I used to just kick for fun beginning when I was nine. That was the first time I did it for an organized team. Ever since then, 1978, I've been fortunate to still be in it all this time."

He noted numerous reasons for his consistently high level of NFL success.

"It's been a combination of a lot of things—I've been very lucky, have had a lot of good people around me, you have to get some breaks,"

Landeta said. "There are a lot of reasons why I ended up being a punter professionally. I've never taken it for granted and always appreciated everything that came with it. I think that's also helped me stay around."

While Landeta points to a multitude of factors for his lengthy career, one man in particular stands out.

"The guy responsible for me playing today was my high school coach, Ben Petrelli," Landeta stated. "If he didn't invite me to come out my senior year, I would have never played. I'm very grateful to him and he's aware of it.

"He's the reason why I'm playing all these years."

Landeta punted and kicked in high school and at Towson State, where he led Division II in punting from 1980-82. In 1980, he became the first kicker ever to lead D-II in both punting (43.4-yard average) and kicking, with 14 field goals. However, it quickly became apparent to Landeta what form of booting he would have to do to reach the next level.

"I used to do both, but I was not accurate enough on field goals," he laughed. "I was only a 50-percent field goal kicker. But my punting was good enough to be at the pro level."

It was a wise decision, to say the least.

THE GAME OF MY LIFE
GIANTS VS. REDSKINS—NFC CHAMPIONSHIP, JANUARY 11, 1987
BY SEAN LANDETA

The best game I ever had statistically was a preseason game against the Patriots in 1987. I don't think I ever had a game where I had five punts in a row that were all between 52 and 59 yards in one game. Statistically that was the best, but that would certainly not be my best game ever; that would be the NFC Championship Game against the Redskins in January of 1987. I think that was probably my best game, especially because the conditions were so bad.

I was very lucky that day to make really good contact on all six of my kicks (for a 42.3-yard average). Those were probably the worst conditions I've ever played in. The wind chill was about zero with 35-mph winds. I got lucky that I was able to hit almost every ball just right.

If I tried to do that in practice on six punts in a row, I probably couldn't do it.

I honestly always tried to approach playoff games the same as I did preseason and regular-season games. I just tried to go out and punt the ball as best as I could and not pay attention to what the game was labeled. I know a lot of players say that, but for me that was really the truth.

When the weather is that bad, you basically just try to do everything the same. Fortunately for us, we had most of December and into January to practice in that weather. Getting that practice time helped out a lot. It was obviously very difficult, but I was lucky when it came to game time that I hit them all so well.

None of the kicks really stand out in particular, but I knew there were some good ones in that game. Obviously some weren't as good as the others, but considering the conditions it worked out pretty well.

I can recall the whole season we won our first Super Bowl. It seemed like each game—from preseason to the Super Bowl—we went out, we practiced, we got ready and played and that was it. We just went about each week very business-like. We'd go out, play well and win, which allowed us to do the same the next week. It's kind of hard to explain but that's how it was. There was nothing fancy or out of the ordinary that entire season.

I remember all the confetti flying around Giants Stadium after the game. That was such a great moment. I remember I didn't run right into the locker room afterwards and just sat on the bench and watched the fans. I told myself to just take it all in because something like this might not come around again. It was really just a great, great time. Everybody was real happy and there were a lot of guys in the locker room yelling and hollering. It was great. It was really wonderful.

After the game, when we were at the party at the hotel, we were already talking about going back to the Super Bowl the next season. It's only normal to think that way because we had the same team coming back. But we didn't get back until four years later. After you get there and don't get back, you really realize how difficult it is and how many things have to happen for you to be able to do it.

Looking back on it now, a part of you wishes that you had enjoyed it even more. Not that you didn't enjoy it at the time, but if we could go back in time to when great things happen for us, we should enjoy it as much as possible because you just don't know if and when it'll happen again.

Everybody got along on that team and everybody treated each other well, it didn't matter what position you played. That was before free agency so guys stayed on the same team for a while. That was a really good group of guys.

Another great game I had, considering the conditions, was the playoff game in Chicago the year before. The wind chill was below zero. I had a minus-six-yard punt in that game, the one I grazed off the side of my foot. But also in that game, I had three punts inside the 10. I had a 63-yard punt and a 54-yard punt. Except for that one freak play, I hit all the other punts very well. I probably averaged 42 yards on those other punts. I'm sure no one remembers any of the good ones, though. Even so, that was probably my next best game.

And while the Redskins game was definitely my best game, my best punt came in Super Bowl XXV. With a little more than two minutes left, we pinned Buffalo just inside the 10-yard line. They ended up driving down and tried to make that late field goal. Looking back, that was probably the most important punt that I've had to hit. If I kick it in the end zone, maybe they're 10 yards closer. Or, if I don't hit it that well, they might be able to run it back. But we got a fair catch just inside the 10, which was obviously a good time to hit a good one.

GAME RESULTS

Field position was so much a part of this contest that when Giants captain Harry Carson won the pregame coin toss, he and his club opted to take the wind, instead of the ball. It was that kind of day. Winds up to 35 mph whipped the Giants Stadium faithful into a frenzy and frigid temperatures rendered any sort of sustained offensive attack punch-less for both sides.

The Giants got on the board first, using the gusts to their advantage, as Raul Allegre drilled a wind-aided 47-yard field goal. New York used the same recipe on its next possession. With the wind at his back, Phil Simms hooked up with Lionel Manuel for a 25-yard gain to convert a third-and-20, and then connected with Manuel again for an 11-yard touchdown and an insurmountable 10-0 lead. The Giants extended their edge to 17-0 when Joe Morris barreled over from one yard out in the second quarter.

New York only converted a dozen first downs and passed for 82 yards all game long, but it was more than enough.

The rest was up to Sean Landeta and the defense. With Washington kicker Steve Cox struggling to master the tricky Meadowlands winds, Landeta averaged 42.3 yards per boot on six kicks, an unfathomable figure given the conditions. Continually pinned deep by Landeta and facing a 17-0 deficit for the entire second half, Redskins quarterback Jay Schroeder threw 50 times and only gained 195 yards through the air.

"Obviously it was extremely windy and field position was key in that game," Giants President/CEO John Mara recalled.

It all added up to a wild scene that ended with the New York Football Giants heading to the Super Bowl for the first time in franchise history.

Chapter 5

MATT BAHR

THE YOUNG LIFE OF MATT BAHR

There was never any question that Matt Bahr was going to be a professional sports star—the only uncertainty was in which sport he would excel. Bahr comes from soccer royalty. His father, Walter, is a member of the National Soccer Hall of Fame.

"My dad played on that (United States) World Cup team that beat England, 1-0, in 1950, in Brazil," Bahr recounts. "They beat England in a big upset. It's still talked about as one of the biggest upsets in the world of soccer. My father took the shot and had the assist on the only goal. My dad was a world-class soccer player."

Bahr's two brothers, Casey and Chris, weren't too shabby on the soccer fields either; Casey was a participant in the infamous 1972 Olympics.

"He was pretty much coming back into the compound when the shootings started between the Palestinians and the Israelis," Bahr said. "He knew something was up the next morning when his room was busted into by security because they were trying to get (U.S. swimmer) Mark Spitz out of there."

Growing up, soccer was clearly what Bahr knew best—and was also the source of his greatest joy. But it wasn't until his father shared his incredible insight with his two youngest sons did Matt's career path change.

"We had all come from a soccer background," he said. "Chris and I also played pro soccer in the old NASL. My father saw very early on that eventually all kickers would be soccer style. He thought we should try out (for football), but our problem was we never wanted to give up playing soccer to kick footballs. In high school (Neshaminy Langhorne High School in Langhorne, Pennsylvania), I'd practice on Tuesday nights and kick on Friday nights. At Penn State, we would kick with the center and holder before practice, I'd jog over to soccer practice, and then if Joe (Paterno) wanted to kick field goals with the team he'd let me know and I'd jog back over after soccer practice.

"Joe didn't like it, but that's kind of the way it was."

Simply put, the regimented Paterno dealt with it because Bahr was that good.

Bahr was good enough on both fronts that in 1978 he even played a little pro soccer with the Colorado Caribous of the now-defunct NASL while still a Penn State student.

"You used to be able to play pro soccer in the spring and Penn State football in the fall," he laughed. "I was playing soccer and football, pro and amateur, in the same year."

Soon, Bahr's tremendously accurate leg landed him in the NFL, where he toiled for 17 seasons.

"I think one of the reasons I kicked so long was because I worked during the day in the off-season and went to school at night," Bahr stated. "One of the reasons for the longevity was that I never felt like I needed to play football to earn a living."

THE GAMES OF MY LIFE
GIANTS AT 49ERS—NFC CHAMPIONSHIP, JANUARY 20, 1991; GIANTS VS. BILLS—SUPER BOWL XXV, JANUARY 27, 1991
BY MATT BAHR

In both the NFC Championship Game and the Super Bowl, we were big underdogs and needed every single play to just barely win. And

---

Matt Bahr kicks one of the most important field goals of his career during Super Bowl XXV against the Buffalo Bills.
Rick Stewart, Getty Images

I really mean every single play—and everyone contributed to it. We were a good team, but the teams we beat—the 49ers were going for the three-peat and Buffalo was scoring 8,000 points a game—were real good. We were touchdown underdogs in both of those games.

The reason the Super Bowl stands out in my mind a little bit more is not even for the field goals, or the field goal at the end, but being able to make two tackles in that game. I did something that no one expected me to do. For me, that was a great thrill to be able to say I was part of two tackles in the Super Bowl. I know in talking to some of the Buffalo players after the game they realized they would have been touchdowns had I not made the tackles. People still say stuff to me about it to this day. Not so much about the kick, but they'll talk about, "That tackle you made that saved seven points." When you look at it that way, at least for me, that's one of the nicer compliments I can receive.

I remember thinking as those two plays were unfolding, "I had better make this." It's a desperation borne out of the fact that I'm certainly never going to chase anybody down. So if I can get my hands on them, I better do everything possible to retain a grip and eventually drag them down. I got a couple pats on the back because I made a good play. The whole game was like that. The extraordinary became ordinary. Guys were really playing well and we needed to. Both San Francisco and Buffalo were such strong teams that every play had an impact on the outcome.

I was never one to lose much sleep before big games. That's the "big test syndrome." I was always able to get a good night's sleep because not doing so was a bad thing. I always slept comfortably. It's like when a team would call a timeout before a kick, that's about the best thing they could do for me. In San Francisco, they had just re-sodded the whole field and the turf was real loose; you could see it coming up from under guys' feet. When they called a timeout it was great. It gave me a chance to check the footing and find a good area from which to kick.

Steve DeOssie, who was our long-snapper, likes to tell this story, which I don't remember, but I'm willing to go with Steve's account. When they called the timeout before the kick in San Francisco, he came back to the huddle and said, "They can't ice you." I said, "Steve, they're not trying to ice me, they're trying to ice you."

One of the things about kicking the game-winner is that it's very much like being a golfer. You know when you've hit the ball well as soon as it's off your foot. As soon as it came off my foot, I said, "Boy, I hit that ball good." Then I said, "Uh-oh, I hope I didn't hit it too good." It hugged the inside left upright, which, as it turns out, was the best thing that could have happened. With the rush they had on, had it been down the middle they would have blocked it. It was a great scheme on their rush; you can see it on the tape. You can see their guy (Spencer Tillman) leaping through the middle of the line. They lined three guys outside the wing. The two most inside of those three guys took the wing and the end and the far outside guy ran across their backs and dove through a hole that opened up in the middle of the line. It was really a well-thought out rush and he timed it perfectly. He was right where the ball would have gone had I hit it right up the middle.

Let me share what I think was one of the more interesting things that happened to me in my career. I broke in my rookie season with the great Steelers teams that won four Super Bowls in six seasons. I was a rookie coming to the defending Super Bowl champions. The first game is on a Monday night up in New England, and my first game is about to be my last game. I had missed a field goal and an extra point. Howard Cosell was already writing my epitaph. It really could have, and probably should have, been my last game.

But then it was 13-13 in overtime. In the eight weeks I had been around that team, Jack Lambert had not said even one word to me. During the timeout before my kick, here comes Jack Lambert walking toward me and I'm thinking to myself, "Well this can't be good." He gets back to me and says, "Matt, we have all the confidence in the world in you." Now I don't know if that helped me make the field goal or not, but I always admired him for that.

Pretty much the exact same thing happened when I was with the Giants. I had only been there a few weeks and we had a game-winning kick against the Cardinals in Giants Stadium (a 20-19 victory on October 21, 1990). You might not believe this, because he never stops talking, but Lawrence Taylor still had not said a word to me in the whole time I was there. They called a timeout to ice the kicker, and he said to me, "You take all the time you want; we'll keep them out of there." They were the first words he ever said to me; it was almost exactly the same as with Jack Lambert. To me, that's what made them great players. They had great individual ability—they changed the game—but they were also great teammates. They wanted everyone around them to be the best that they could be. That's always meant a lot to me.

In both of those situations in those two games, they were win-lose situations. It wasn't a tie; it wasn't to tie it up to go into overtime. It was you're either going to win it or you're going to lose it. I don't know how often that's happened in NFL history, during a championship game or the Super Bowl. When you're kicking and it's tied up you know in the back of your mind that it's tied up. It's not a case of, "If I miss this, we're going home." Whether that helps or hurts I don't know, but it's certainly a much different type of kick. In each case—in each game—it was a change-of-lead situation.

But I never looked at pressure that way. I always looked at it like you've got nothing to lose and everything to gain. Just take a deep breath, forget everything you were ever taught, keep your head down and kick through the ball. You really have to reduce it to the basics. You can't control the situation, you can't control the crowd, you can't control what the other team is going to do. So why worry about it?

So we hit the winner in San Francisco, and now instead of taking the plane back to New York, we took the plane right to Florida. Since there was only a week in between games, we had packed for the Super Bowl, in case we actually made it.

In the Super Bowl, I was hoping for anything else to happen other than him (Scott Norwood) having to miss that kick. I was rooting for a bad snap, a bad hold, an interception or a fumble, anything so that the onus wouldn't be on the kicker. I wanted anything to happen so it didn't have to be a missed field goal.

Everyone reduces that game to just that kick. And the game was so much more than just that kick. It's an injustice to all the great plays and players in that game—Mark Ingram's catch-and-run on third down, Jeff Hostetler holding onto the ball in the end zone to give up two points and not seven points. Every single player came up with a play like that—and on both teams. Shane Conlan came up with some unbelievable tackles in that game. I didn't think we'd ever stop Thurman Thomas. He was phenomenal. To have it end because of a mistake does a disservice to how good those players were.

Believe it or not, and this goes for most guys that I talk to, it's more fun to win the championship game than the Super Bowl. When you win the championship game, you're going to the Super Bowl. When you win the Super Bowl, it's like, "Ok, who do we play next?" You don't want the feeling to end. You want to keep playing because winning is so much of a thrill. Yes, you win the Super Bowl and it's a definite thrill. But I really think you're more enthusiastic winning the championship game.

GAME RESULTS

The Giants and 49ers had been neck-and-neck all game long, and the Niners, who were driving in Giants territory, held the slimmest of leads, 13-12, with less than three minutes to play. That was until Erik Howard slammed into Roger Craig and forced a fumble that Lawrence Taylor recovered. A couple clutch throws from Jeff Hostetler later and the Giants—and Matt Bahr—were lining up for the game-winning kick.

As Bahr pointed out, the 49ers' attempt to ice him actually worked in his favor—as did the fact that he didn't hit the ball as perfectly as he had hoped. That allowed the pigskin to squeeze by Spencer Tillman, who had gotten a great rush and was in perfect position to block the kick. Bahr's 42-yarder snuck inside the left upright as time expired and the Giants were headed to the Super Bowl for the second time in five seasons.

"To me, Matt was the star of that game," Giants President/CEO John Mara said. "I remember thinking that there was no one else I would rather have attempt that last kick. I sat in a suite behind the goal post in the direction he was kicking, and when it went through that was as great an ending to one of our games as I had ever experienced—until the next week, of course."

That next week, once again Bahr's leg provided the final margin of victory; he drilled a 21-yard field goal with 7:20 to play.

"I recall Matt very calmly kicking what turned out to be the game-winning field goal to put us ahead by a point in the fourth quarter," Giants punter Sean Landeta said.

However, it was Bahr's toughness and determination that allowed New York to stay close to the powerful Bills earlier in the contest. The 5-foot-10, 165-pound Bahr made two enormous special-teams tackles in that game. In both instances, had he not found a way to drag down the Buffalo returner, the Bills certainly would have scored a touchdown. First, he denied the Bills a chance to jump to an early lead when he stopped Don Smith on the opening kickoff. Then in the third quarter, he was able to bring down Al Edwards, narrowly averting disaster once again.

We all know how arguably the most exciting Super Bowl in NFL history ended—with Scott Norwood missing a 47-yarder wide right on the game's final play, claiming for New York the Lombardi Trophy once again.

"I remember, after the game in the locker room how happy we all were and with Matt's locker being next to mine, just us really enjoying that great moment in our football lives," Landeta said.

That capped a two-game stretch that no player—kicker or otherwise—will likely ever see again.

Chapter 6

STEPHEN BAKER

THE YOUNG LIFE OF STEPHEN BAKER

Give credit where credit is due. That wonderful nickname—Stephen Baker, the Touchdown Maker—that fans and media alike ate up came from none other than Stephen Baker himself.

After yet another multi-touchdown performance for Hamilton High School in Los Angeles, Baker asked the reporter if he could refer to himself in that regard.

"I used to call myself Stephen Baker, the Touchdown Maker long before the media and fans started using it," Baker laughed. "I used to score six or seven touchdowns every time we played street ball."

Baker's gridiron start came playing street ball, when he and fellow youngsters would play football without pads during halftime of the Pop Warner games.

"There were no weight or age restrictions," Baker recalled. "That helped me when I got to high school. The first time I got tackled I couldn't believe how soft it felt with all those pads on."

It didn't take Baker long to make an impact at the high school level. Baker, who had lost his mouthpiece earlier in practice, was next up in a tackling drill. However, once his coach realized he was without a mouth guard, Baker was told he would be unable to take part in the drill. That's when Baker took matters into his own hands—and mouth.

"I was about to get thrown out of a drill because I lost my mouthpiece," he said. "I turned around and snatched the mouthpiece out of the mouth of the kid behind me and I did the drill. Even though it was disgusting, I think the coach knew I was going to be a player from that point on."

The beginning of Baker's high school and college careers were mirror images. In his first game as a member of Hamilton's freshman team, Baker was open in the end zone and about to collect the game-winning pass as the clock expired for his first-ever score. Not so fast. The ball bounced off his chest but fortunately right into the outstretched hands of a teammate who collected the ball to avert disaster.

However, it didn't take Baker long to bounce back. The next week he took a reverse 65 yards and scored during an organized football game for the first time in his life

"That was the turning point of my football career," Baker said. "I started varsity as a sophomore and never looked back."

It wasn't much longer until Baker threw a four-spot on the scoreboard.

"I scored four TDs in a game right after I found out my uncle had passed away," Baker said. "I didn't even want to play, but I said a prayer and went out and scored four TDs. That's when the press got hold of the name. I didn't realize it seemed like a cocky thing to do."

At West Los Angeles Junior College, Baker became an end-zone regular. But there would be another bump in the football road for Baker. After scoring 31 touchdowns in his two years at West L.A., which also boasted Warren Moon and Keyshawn Johnson as alums, Baker begin his career at Fresno State.

"My first game at Fresno State, just like in high school, I ran a slant route and I dropped the ball," he painfully recalled. "After the game, someone wrote, 'Stephen Baker, the Touchdown Faker.' But the next week at Oregon State I caught a 98-yarder. After that, it was curtains.

"You have to know how to bounce back from adversity. If I had been a weak-minded individual, I never would have made it."

Baker also excelled in the punt return game, taking back his first ever punt 80 yards to the house.

While most athletes sharpen their skills on the playgrounds and streets while growing up, Baker's mother, Lucille, took a different approach to raising Stephen and his brother, Terrence.

Stephen Baker, the Touchdown Maker, scored 21 touchdowns in six seasons with the Giants. *Rick Stewart, Getty Images*

"Believe it or not, she raised us with video games to keep us in the house," he said. "We always had top-of-the-line games. It kept us inside and out of the bad areas."

But once Baker became too good to keep off the football field, Mom was behind him all the way.

"She'd come to every game she could when she wasn't working," he said. "My mom was very instrumental in my career."

THE GAME OF MY LIFE
GIANTS AT REDSKINS—OCTOBER 14, 1990
BY STEPHEN BAKER

The game of my life came against the Redskins at RFK Stadium. The big play of that game was a third-and-10 in the second quarter. Eric Moore had just jumped offsides so it was third-and-10 from our own 20.

The crowd was going crazy. We called a simple route we had been calling all year called, "Y and X cross." It's just a six-yard route by the receiver with a natural pick of his defender. (Phil) Simms made a great throw, (David) Meggett made a great block and it went for 80 yards. You could hear a pin drop in that stadium. We won a huge game and that was definitely the play that sparked us. That had to be my favorite game.

I could tell they were playing man defense right away because we sent Mark Ingram in motion and of course (Redskins CB) Darrell Green went with him. So I knew all I had to do was beat my man. Stacy (Robinson) went over the top and I went underneath him. We wanted the defenders to rub off on each other. Simms made the throw and I just made sure to concentrate on the ball. I couldn't worry about where guys were or if I was going to get hit. I always jumped when I caught the ball and Simms put it right into my breadbasket.

I remember seeing Lionel (Manuel) backside locked up with his man because he was running a deep comeback. I knew from watching film and watching Stacy run that route so many times that as soon as you caught the ball you had to turn it straight up the field. That way, by the time the defender came off Lionel, it was too late for him to get you. At that point, the only guy that could catch you is the guy trailing you (Brian Davis). But you always knew in the back of your mind that Darrell Green was looming.

Most people don't understand that when you break into the clear, you can't run fast enough. It's like being in a bad dream and you're trying to run, but it feels like you're running in quicksand. The end zone can't come soon enough. I also never looked back. I was always taught to never look back. During that game, Maurice Carthon had a big, 63-yard gain and Mark Bavaro also went 61 yards. Both of those guys looked back and both ended up getting caught from behind.

I didn't look back one time. I learned that from running track. Whenever you're in a race, you never turn around to see who's behind you because you lose a tenth of a second every time you do. That followed me into football. And to me, if you look back, you're questioning your own speed. I knew that if I got a lead on someone, they weren't going to catch me.

After I scored, I saw a couple Redskins fans giving me the finger. I remember the whole stadium being silent but looking over at our sideline and everyone was going nuts. Stacy and Lionel were always the first to come over to pick me up and hug me. To me, scoring touchdowns on the road was more enjoyable than scoring touchdowns at home, because it was just you and your teammates.

I still have the tape of that game at home and you can hear John Madden saying that I ran about 135 yards on that play. I had to run from one hash to the other and then turn it up all the way. To run that far for that long with a ball in your hand is very exhausting.

I gave that touchdown ball to my father. I always kept the first touchdown ball I scored every season and gave it to him. It's at home in Los Angeles sitting up on the mantle.

That was the year we started 10-0. It was the fifth game of the season and it was my first start of the season. Odessa Turner had gotten hurt so I went in for him. To come out in that fashion and do that was great. I was always trying to prove myself to Bill Parcells that I could play. He had always told me that he knew that I could play, but he doubted whether or not I could endure a whole 16-game season. So I always went into games with a chip on my shoulder, thinking, "Let me show this man I can play some ball." Going into that game I was very excited; I just wanted to prove what I could do. That was the story of my whole career. As you could imagine, I often heard throughout my career that I was too small, that I couldn't do it.

I felt fine going into that game. I honestly never really got nervous except for the first game that I ever played. In practice every day I went up against Perry Williams and Mark Collins. Those two, to me, were some of the best corners in the league. When I got into games, it felt like it was easy. I'm not trying to discredit the competition, but I really never thought that anybody could cover me.

Right after I went 80 yards, we had the ball again right before the half and we were driving again. They threw me a bomb and it just went off the ends of my fingertips. Then I had to run a deep out and I was dead tired. A couple plays later I ran a slant. By this time, the Redskins had more than enough of Stephen Baker, the Touchdown Maker. The safety came up and totally cleaned my clock out. The half ended and I went back into the locker room. I suffered a concussion. I remember kneeling right by Parcells and throwing up on his foot. I'm thinking, "He's definitely going to get rid of me now." But I couldn't help it; I was concussed.

I really don't remember much of the second half. I don't believe I caught a pass after halftime, but I very well might have and don't even remember it. All I do remember is getting hit and not knowing where I was and then throwing up on his shoe. He didn't say anything; he just moved out of the way really fast. One of the players went to get trainer Ronnie Barnes to come get me. Wow, how embarrassing that was.

That game was huge for us. Parcells always preached to take it one game at a time. So to be able to jump out on our big rivals like that was huge. Parcells' first words to me when he drafted me were that I have to hate the Redskins—not just dislike, but hate them. The coolest thing was when we played them again and they introduced me at Giants Stadium; that was probably the loudest roar I ever received. Those games were played only two weeks apart. And then to score on the same guy (Davis) again was extra special. He was so frustrated that he nailed me in the back after I scored. I did a front flip and threw the ball up in the air. William Roberts and Bavaro came to my defense, which was really cool.

Another very memorable game for me was the night game in New Orleans in 1988. I had my longest-ever catch, an 85-yarder. It was a simple bomb route that Coach Tom (Coughlin) had taught us how to run a little differently than I had in the past. Jeff Hostetler made a great throw. Once again, shutting up a huge crowd, especially in a dome, was unbelievable. I caught a pass with three seconds to play and Bjorn Nittmo kicked the game-winner (in a 13-12 victory). I was on top of the world after that one.

Of course, the Super Bowl at the end of the '90 season was a great game too. I only had two catches—one was a tip off Howard Cross' fingers. I snatched that one out of the air like a fly. Then of course the touchdown. They had a blitz on and Hostetler made a great pass. He put the ball right out there in the corner. I caught it in the end zone and said, "Now all we have to do is win this game." We did.

GAME RESULTS

The Giants headed down to Washington, D.C. with a 4-0 record. They fought and scrapped before leaving with the victory—their fifth straight of the season and also the fifth consecutive time they knocked off the rival Redskins.

Baker's heroics gave the Giants a 7-3 halftime edge. Bavaro's big catch-and-run set up an Ottis Anderson touchdown run, which extended New York's lead to 14-6. Washington wouldn't quit, however, and sliced the lead to 14-13 on a 31-yard Earnest Byner-to-Ricky Sanders halfback option pass. Again the Giants responded, this time with Carthon's big gain setting up a Bavaro TD grab and it was 21-13 Giants after three.

After the Redskins once again cut into the Giants' lead, Matt Bahr extended Big Blue's cushion to 24-20, a score that stood up after Greg Jackson's late interception iced the game.

All told, Baker finished with three grabs for 109 yards and the game's most critical touchdown.

"I recall Stephen Baker as an undersized player with a lot of heart who had a knack for making big plays and scoring touchdowns," Giants President/CEO John Mara said. "He scored a big TD for us in the Super Bowl that year as well."

Chapter 7

JOE MORRIS

THE YOUNG LIFE OF JOE MORRIS

Joe Morris displayed his knack of capitalizing on big opportunities from a very young age. When Morris was in the third grade, his father, Earl, a Green Beret and 28-year veteran of the U.S. Army, was serving in Vietnam. That's when Morris snuck in the question that would change his life—and that of Giants fans as well.

"This is how I got my chance to play," Morris laughed. "My dad was in Vietnam at the time and every once in a while, he'd call and we'd all get a chance to talk to him for just a quick minute or two. For my two minutes, I said, 'Dad, can I play football?' He said, 'Yes, son, you can play football. Put your mom on the phone.'"

And the rest is history.

"He told my mom (Addie) to let me play football," Morris recalled. "And that's how I got my chance to play. Trust me, my mom would never let me play football until my dad gave his word. I took my shot and it worked."

Morris began his gridiron career playing guard and defensive tackle. Needless to say, that didn't last long.

"I was the fastest guy on the team so I moved to running back the next year," he said.

By the time he was a freshman at Syracuse University, Morris had impressed at least one influential man—Orange head coach Frank Maloney.

"He told me when I was just a freshman that I had some ability and that I was going to play in the NFL one day," Morris stated. "I was thinking to myself, 'Yeah, whatever.' I didn't think I'd be playing anywhere but Syracuse. He knew it then so I owe a lot to him."

After smashing several Syracuse rushing marks by surpassing 4,000 career yards, Morris was New York's second-round pick in the 1982 Draft.

"Then, when I did make it, I figured I'd be playing two or three years, tops," he recounted. "Then I had a nine-year career. I always thought I'd be a teacher."

NFL defenses wish he had ended up in the classroom.

THE GAMES OF MY LIFE
GIANTS VS. REDSKINS—OCTOBER 27, 1986;
GIANTS VS. COWBOYS—NOVEMBER 2, 1986
BY JOE MORRIS

During our Super Bowl season I had 181 yards against Washington and 181 yards against Dallas in back-to-back weeks. Those two games especially stand out in my mind. Many of our receivers were hurt, so we had to run the ball to win. We played Washington on Monday night and then played Dallas the following Sunday. It was quite a week for me. I also scored two touchdowns in each game.

I clearly remember what Bill Parcells said to me before those games. He told me that I had to pick it up, that we didn't have our receivers, and that he was going to have to rely on me. Then he asked me if I thought I could handle it. I told him I would do whatever I could. We were playing our two biggest rivals and all the coach is asking is that I give him my best effort. Since I always did, that was easy enough. After those games, with all the numbers I put up, I felt content that I did all that I could have.

Parcells always told me that I didn't realize how good I could be and that we weren't going to know that until all the receivers got back. Until then, we were just going to do what we had to do to win. We needed to win both of those games to maintain our position in the standings and Parcells always knew exactly how to motivate us. You never thought he

---

Joe Morris rushed for more than 1,000 yards three times during his seven years in New York. *Ronald C. Modra, Getty Images*

was asking too much out of you, just the most you could give. It was easy for me to give my all because I was so sick of losing. Those two games were so important for our drive to the Super Bowl.

I can still see those two opponents in my mind. I remember all the players, all the defenses, and all the plays. I still remember a lot from our meetings before those games. I had such respect for the Washington Redskins. I never hated the Redskins; they always played hard and clean. There was never any dirty stuff from them. But the Cowboys? Man, I hated the Cowboys.

I used to keep notes on all the linebackers we played and I remember filling my notebook with all the stuff the Redskins and Cowboys linebackers used to try to do to me. But the best thing about those games was that everyone knew I was getting the ball; they knew we had to run it and they still couldn't stop it. (Tight end) Mark Bavaro, (offensive lineman) Karl Nelson and (fullback) Maurice Carthon made my job so much easier.

The weirdest thing about those games was that I had a fan in Dallas who sent me a tape of the games a week later. It was definitely the weirdest thing I've ever gotten in the mail. He had taped both games and he sent it to me in the mail along with some items he wanted me to sign. It was weird to see myself on TV like that. I'm still not totally sure why the guy sent me the tape, but it sure was nice. I always watched a lot of tape when I played, but to watch the TV coverage of my games and to hear John Madden and whoever else talking about me was definitely much different.

The funniest thing I saw on the tape was how much shorter I was than everyone else. When I was playing in the games, I obviously wasn't aware of it. And of course watching the games I saw plays where I should have cut here or should have gone there.

Both of those teams ran 4-3 fronts. When you're playing against those types of defenses, you had better be prepared and bring your best. There were so many good players on both of those defenses.

We were a game out of first place heading into the Washington game and knew we had to win. It was a Monday night game and we knew how important it was. That was the night that the Mets won the World Series. Guys on our team were upset because the fans were cheering for the Mets during our game. I remember that we had to score late to win. We drove down, got near the end zone and then I was able to take it in from there. We played our hearts out and won a huge game.

I scored the touchdown late, but they still had some time to come back on us. You were thinking at that point that you wished you hadn't left them as much time on the clock as we did. But our defense stepped up and stopped them so we won the game. We were all very happy after that one.

That was some night for New York—we won a huge game and the Mets won the World Series. There was a lot of excitement and hoopla going on. But I still remember clear as day what Parcells said after the game. He right away said, "We have a game on Sunday; we have the Cowboys on Sunday." I remember thinking, "Man, can't we just enjoy this for a minute?"

Once the Dallas game came, it was just time to play football again. Dallas had beaten us the first game of the year, and there was no way they were going to get us again. I remember talking to Parcells before we played them and telling him that Dallas knew exactly what we were going to do. He said he knew that, but they still had to stop it. He said he had confidence in me and our offense. Even though they knew what was coming, it didn't mean they could stop it and we proved they couldn't. That was also a hard-fought game and when we had to run the ball, we were able to run it effectively; the two TDs in that game were both short runs.

I was named player of the week for one of those games. I didn't even know it at the time. Parcells used to try to keep all that stuff quiet and low. I didn't find out until I was looking at a Super Bowl program months later.

After we had lost to Chicago in the playoffs in '85, we vowed that we wanted to get our playoff games at home the next season. To do that, we knew we'd have to win all of our home games, which we did. These two were probably the two toughest and they came back-to-back.

Looking back on it now is really neat. When you know you're playing your biggest rivals, you know you're going to have to step your game up. I was able to do that. I had a lot of help from my teammates, which I was very proud of.

Since the first game was a Monday and the next was the following Sunday, it literally was two games in a week. I had two huge rushing yardage games, scored two TDs in each, and we beat our two biggest rivals. Man, was that ever a great week.

That '86 season was magical. I really came into my own then. Parcells admitted being surprised about some of the things I could do on the football field. What most people don't realize about that year is that I missed a game. When Tiki (Barber) broke my Giants' single-season rushing yardage mark, he only did so by a few yards and he had an extra game. I had some fluke reaction to some medication and I missed the fourth game of the season.

The other reason I remember '86 so fondly is because that was the year that my daughter was born. We were playing the Eagles that weekend, but all I was worried about was scoring a touchdown for my new daughter Samantha and bringing the ball to the hospital for her. Samantha being born really made it a special year.

There is one other game that I have to mention. It came in 1984, when I first started playing regularly. We were playing Kansas City at home and we scored two touchdowns at the end of the game to win. The fans were leaving the game and booing us because we were losing. We pulled the game out, 28-27. We scored two touchdowns in the final nine minutes. I was just starting to play and I helped us score those two late TDs. I was really proud of that game. Now, I'm not crazy enough to say that fans can't boo and shouldn't show their frustration, because I totally understood them—we stunk the joint out for most of the game.

I remember in the huddle I was talking about how they were booing us. Phil Simms said, "Joe, I don't give a damn what they're doing out there. We have to win this game." That game was really the beginning of the team starting to mature and come together.

GAME RESULTS

While the hearts, minds, and eyes of most Giants fans were on Game 7 of the World Series, the Giants were able to knock off the Redskins, 27-20, and claim a share of first place they would never relinquish.

Redskins receiver Gary Clark may have won the battle, but Joe Morris and his Giants captured this all-important war. Clark torched New York's secondary, gaining 241 yards on 11 catches. But Morris countered with 181 ground yards (on 31 carries) to go with another 59 through the air to total 240 yards of damage himself. And it was his 13-

yard TD run with 1:38 to play that proved to be Big Blue's final margin of victory.

Only six days later, New York brought home its second enormous victory of the week. The Giants faithful held their collective breath as Rafael Septien's 63-yard field goal attempt fell well short with 18 seconds to play, securing a 17-14 New York win.

For the second straight week, Morris accounted for 181 yards (this time on 29 carries) and two TDs (8 and 6 yards)—and for the second contest in a row he finished one yard shy of the opposition's offensive star. Dallas running back Herschel Walker tore through New York's defense for 182 all-purpose yards.

But the Giants defense—led by Harry Carson's 13 tackles and nine more from Carl Banks, including a pair of sacks—was once again able to hang on at the end to put another hard-fought victory on ice.

Chapter 8

JIM FASSEL

THE YOUNG LIFE OF JIM FASSEL

Like most aspiring young athletes, Jim Fassel's father, Bud, played a huge role in his ascension and development as a quarterback, then coach. However, Fassel pointed to one of his former coaches for really showing him the coaching ropes.

"The guy that really steered me into coaching was Hal Sherbeck, the head coach at Fullerton Community College," explained Fassel, who also played quarterback at USC and Long Beach State. "I played for him and started coaching for him. He helped me get started. He was kind of my mentor. I always looked at him as a guy that I followed. I was always close to Hal and he influenced me a lot."

But it wasn't until Fassel actually saw Sherbeck in action that he knew he wanted to emulate his mentor.

"I always looked at him and respected him as a coach," Fassel said. "I looked at his lifestyle and his passion about coaching and I said, 'That's what I want to do.'"

However, becoming a head coach on the pro level was a daunting enough task that Fassel, who was a seventh-round pick of the Bears in 1972, never really thought he had what it took until several years later.

"I never got into coaching thinking I was going to be a head coach in the NFL," he said. "I never thought about it. I dreamed about it when I was in college and thought what a great job that would be. I was always just focused on whatever job I had at the time.

"Even when I came into the league as an assistant with the Giants (as QBs coach in 1991) I still wasn't sure that it would ever happen. But after my first year at Denver (1993) I thought that I could definitely be a head coach in this league. After my second year, I was very confident of it."

Obviously, his confidence was well-founded.

THE GAMES OF MY LIFE

GIANTS VS. EAGLES—NFC DIVISIONAL PLAYOFF, JANUARY 7, 2001;
GIANTS VS. VIKINGS—NFC CHAMPIONSHIP GAME, JANUARY 14, 2001
BY JIM FASSEL

The two games that stand out in my mind are the playoff game against the Eagles and the championship game against the Vikings on our march to the Super Bowl.

First, with the Eagles, we had beaten those guys eight straight times—for four straight years we beat them twice. They were all good, hard-fought games. I just remember going into that game thinking that this is the most pressure-packed game that I've ever coached because of the circumstances. We were having a real good year and were on target to do some good things. We had the home-field advantage for the playoffs—any time you have that there is automatically a ton of pressure on you. Now, if you lose, you've blown it.

Here was a team that had all the motivation in the world to come in and beat us. It was rubbed in the Eagles' face how long it had been since they had beaten us, and they were coming off a pretty good year themselves. If we lose that game, I'm thinking in my mind that all hell's going to break loose around here. A lot of people couldn't handle that very well.

We had fought our way to this opportunity and had to take advantage of it. It was a heck of a hard-fought game. I knew how good they were. Andy Reid had them ready to play.

I worked the guys pretty good, but the most important thing that week was that I needed the players to realize that I wasn't taking the

---

Head coach Jim Fassel holds up the NFC Championship trophy after defeating the Minnesota Vikings 41-0 on January 14, 2001. *AP Image*

Eagles lightly. There's a fine line between overdoing it and wearing them out and giving them too much leeway. We had an extra week off so I kind of took that week and gave them some down time while laying the groundwork in a less intense environment. Everything we did, I held the line all the time to make sure that they didn't see anything from me that would make them think that I was taking anything for granted at all. My focus that whole week was as much on the game plan as it was on the mental state of my team. I had to make it different. And I thought the players focused in really well.

We ran the opening kickoff back for a touchdown. And as excited as I was for that to happen, that's often a kiss of death, especially when you're playing at home. You have a tendency to relax, and I didn't want that to happen. I was working the sideline hard and getting in guys' faces about a bunch of different things.

Before the game I was worried about my team taking the Eagles a little lightly. We had beaten them so many times in a row that it was hard not to think, "Oh yeah, we'll get these guys. We beat them all the time." Then we returned the opening kickoff and I thought, "Oh man, there goes all the work I did all week." I could tell some of the guys, especially the young guys, were thinking, "See, we got these guys." But you know if you even take a deep breath for a second, they'll go up on you and they're hard to come back on.

To me, that game was even more pressure-packed than the game the next week. If you get beat in the championship game, it's obviously not good. But it's also not like losing to a division team that you always beat.

Then we moved on to the championship game. I looked at my team and realized that only a few of them had ever played in that type of game, so I wasn't sure how they'd react.

As we started to prepare for the Vikings, it was obvious that they had an explosive offense with (Daunte) Culpepper, (Randy) Moss, and (Cris) Carter. They were good. I didn't think—as good as our defense was—that we could just go out there and try to milk the clock on them. And I also thought that their weakness on defense was their secondary. But the normal school of thought—and a trap that so many coaches fall into—is to run the football and melt the clock. We didn't take that approach. We said we're going to go after their weakness and, if need be, we'll have to outscore them if our defense doesn't hold them. If they were able to, we thought we could beat them pretty good.

I told every guy on the team that week, "You had better not tell anyone about our game plan. I mean your brothers and sisters, your mom and dad, your wife or girlfriend, and certainly the media, because I'm going to mislead them." I wasn't doing anything wrong—it was just strategy—but I was going to say that we were going to take our time on offense and that we were scared how good their offense was. I went on and on about how careful we had to be with the ball, how critical our run game was going to have to be and how we couldn't afford to get into a shooting match with them. I laid that groundwork all week long, and I remember a lot of the players snickering when they read the papers. But that information was getting to Minnesota, even though the whole time we had planned to come out and jump on them.

I also invited back a lot of former players. I've always believed in bringing players back. Lawrence Taylor, Harry Carson, and George Martin were all there. I asked Lawrence Taylor to say something to the team after practice Saturday, the day before the game. I couldn't have scripted it better. A lot of times when former players come back they talk about how and why they were great, what they did. No one really cares about that. The most important thing Lawrence said—and there must have been at least 30 former players there with him—was that he wanted my team to know that the former players were there to honor them. He said, "We're not here to talk about what we did. We're here for one reason and one reason only—and that's to honor you guys and the season you had." Now if you're a player, you're thinking, "Lawrence Taylor and Harry Carson are going to be watching me." After he finished talking—and usually I say something at that point—I just said, "That's enough boys," and we ended practice.

When we took the field that day, it was the first time I had seen a stadium full for warm-ups. I remember turning to my son on the sideline right before the game. I'm watching the crowd all waving those towels; as for my guys, I could see the stare in their eyes. I turned to my son and said, "They have no chance today." He looked at me and asked, "Are you serious?" I told him to look at the atmosphere and the glare in our guys' eyes. He smiled and said, "You might be right. I sure hope so." And I'm normally not that way. But I knew they had no chance.

The other thing that stands out is when we were strategizing before the game. I always talked to defensive coordinator John Fox. We went through all the usual pregame stuff and then I asked him how many points he thought we'd need to beat the Vikings. He told me he thought we'd need about 34. I thought he was crazy, but that was just him being a coach. After that I teased him about it pretty good. At halftime, it was 34-0. We were walking off the field at halftime and I said, "Ok, John, there's your 34 points." He said, "I know, but they're so good they could still come back." I told him, "If they come back on us we'll both be fired."

I thought we would beat them, but even I didn't think we'd beat them that bad. It was just our day. That's a tough job to try to keep the focus when you're up that much. I remember going in at halftime and telling them they better continue to play hard because I didn't want to see a drop-off. I didn't want to see it get even remotely close. I told the starters that they were going to play a certain amount of time and then I was going to pull them and let the other guys finish it up. I wasn't saying that we were going to go score another 30-something points, but I didn't want to see any sloppy play. They left that locker room ready to go.

Generally as coaches, you only remember the bad games. But those two were so indelible in my mind. The Vikings game was about as enjoyable a game as you're ever going to have. Everyone always wants to have one that they call a laugher where you just play and have fun in the second half without every little thing hurting you. But you still don't want to get anybody hurt or get into sloppy habits. We accomplished all of that.

GAME RESULTS

New York began its 20-10 victory over Philadelphia in the divisional playoffs with a 97-yard kickoff return by rookie Ron Dixon. Two Brad Daluiso field goals sandwiched an athletic, acrobatic 32-yard interception return for a TD by Jason Sehorn, and the Giants defense, which limited the Eagles to 186 yards and 11 first downs, did the rest.

Fassel was able to keep his troops from being overconfident as they knocked off their division rivals for an incredible ninth time in succession.

However, his best coaching job was still to come: Duping the Vikings all week into believing that New York was going to try to play keep-away, then coming out firing on all cylinders from the opening kickoff. By the time Minnesota realized what had hit them, it was too late.

The Giants rolled up 518 yards and 31 first downs, while limiting the Vikings to 114 yards and nine first downs. Kerry Collins threw for 381 yards and five TDs. But Fassel was especially pleased that New York, already up 41-0, heeded his halftime warning and controlled the football for the game's final 12:53.

"Jim did an outstanding job down the stretch in 2000," former Giants GM Ernie Accorsi said. "We were as ready to play technically and emotionally for the Eagles and Vikings under that kind of pressure as any time I have ever seen. Jim was extraordinary."

Chapter 9

LEONARD MARSHALL

THE YOUNG LIFE OF LEONARD MARSHALL

Leonard Marshall is well aware that he never would have reached such athletic heights if not for his parents, Nellie and Leonard.

"I remember my father being very involved in my development," Marshall said. "Both of my parents were very supportive. They were my role models for sure."

Despite being known by friends and family these days as "The Big Cheese," Marshall's modesty and desire to help others are what most stand out about him. For that, he also thanks his folks.

"I got my perseverance from them, as well as my ability to remain grounded and stay humble through the whole process," he recalled. "That still helps me today."

So did the contributions of a few friends and coaches he encountered along the way. While Marshall was at LSU, both Dr. Jack Andonie and defensive line coach Pete Jenkins watched over him and helped keep him in line.

"I didn't get a free education at LSU because it was paid for in exchange for my athletic ability," Marshall said. "But it was guys like Jack Andonie, who's still in New Orleans and does nothing but try to help poor people every day, and Pete Jenkins, who were always in my corner."

Once he reached New York, Marshall toiled under Giants DL coach Lamar Leachman.

"As corny a guy as he was at times, a lot of the stuff he instilled as far as competitiveness, just stayed with me," Marshall stated. "There were a lot of people and things that helped me keep growing as an adolescent and allowed me to keep reinventing myself. That same competitive nature that was instilled a very long time ago is what got me here today."

THE GAME OF MY LIFE
GIANTS VS. BRONCOS—SUPER BOWL XXI, JANUARY 25, 1987
BY LEONARD MARSHALL

I just went out and played every week. The thing I tried to do was make sure that I brought my 'A' game every time I went out to play. But if there was a particular time that I think I shined the brightest it was during championship time. If you go back and look at all the playoff and championship games, if there was one guy on our defense who always brought his 'A' game, it was me.

Championship time was my time. Bill Parcells always used to talk about which players would show up at championship time. He knew in his mind and his heart that if any guys were going to show up for him, he could count on 56 (Lawrence Taylor), 70 (Marshall) and 53 (Harry Carson) for damn sure.

I'm probably most remembered for the 49ers game in 1990, which was an away game. We weren't supposed to be there, and we had a chip on our shoulders because we lost to them on Monday night during the season. Everybody remembers me knocking out Joe Montana in that game. It was a great moment in sports and one that I'll never forget. I'll always hold that memory and my children will always hold that memory.

That was a huge game for me. I had three sacks, seven tackles, and was named defensive player of the month during the playoffs because I had a big game against Chicago the week before and then the big week against Montana and the 49ers. I also got defensive player of the month during the '86 playoffs. People don't remember that. Championship time was my time.

Leonard Marshall won back-to-back NFL Defensive Lineman of the Year honors playing for Big Blue. *George Rose, Getty Images*

But the one game that I remember the most is Super Bowl XXI. I'll always remember George Martin sacking John Elway in the end zone for a safety in Super Bowl XXI. I'll always remember William Roberts and Pepper Johnson doing the stomp-and-grind at midfield after we won that ballgame and the championship. I'll remember my sack on Elway when he was in the open field and was about to break free. I'll always remember hearing, "New York, New York," when we came out for the second half—and we were in California. All those things will never leave me.

I had five members of my family there, and that was obviously the first chance for them to see me play in the Super Bowl. I had a big game against Elway, an unbelievable game to be honest. It was just a great day all around. I took my mother to the Pro Bowl the next week and had a bang-up time. I had never won a SEC or national championship at LSU, so this was the greatest experience and it meant a lot to me.

It was so important to me to have a big game in that situation because that was going to be a moment in time that I could never get back and I realized that. I was only 24 years old at the time, but I realized the magnitude of the situation, and it hit home for me.

I remember joking around with Phil Simms the night before the Super Bowl. His room was right across from mine at the Hilton. Here was a first-round pick who was injured and got picked on at the beginning of his career. I also got picked on early in my career. Now we're here together playing for the world championship. It made a whole lot of sense.

I remember showing up at the stadium four hours before I was supposed to because I was so nervous. I was listening to my Public Enemy CD and just chilling. I was studying my guys, Dave Studdard and Keith Bishop, and trying to figure out what I could do to beat those two guys. My goal was to raise as much hell on their O-line as (Broncos DE) Rulon Jones was going to raise on our O-line. That was my goal. I wanted to make sure they knew they needed to worry about Leonard Marshall and what he was going to do all game long.

That's the mind-set I always had as a player. During my career, I got a chance to talk to guys like Ed "Too Tall" Jones, Richard Dent, and Dexter Manley along the way about what it took for them to become great and dominant players. I always just tried to do the things they did and had success with. You know, like watching a lot of film of your opponent, critiquing yourself more than the others around you, just doing all the little things to make you better. So I had all that in my mind when I went out there for the big game.

The Super Bowl butterflies went away for me even before they announced our names. Before then, I was so tight and nervous. Here I was a young guy and I had to perform right now before 230 million people. How do you like that? How do you like me now? I was a small kid from the Bayou of Louisiana and I was about to play in the country's biggest sporting event. It was incredible.

I remember in the first quarter they were trying to challenge the right side of our defense. They wanted to establish the running game, and LT and I made a pact before the game that if they weren't going to be able to bring it big-time that they weren't going to be able to bring it at all. We let them know right off the bat what it was going to be like. Lawrence and I pretty much shut their run game down very early.

Then they turned around and tried to throw the football against us. So then Lawrence and I put a bunch of pressure on Elway. There was one sack in the game that I actually have a picture of because a fan sent it to me. The picture is of me trying to sack Elway in the middle of the field and Lawrence doing a somersault right over the top of Elway. It was my second sack of the game, but it was a big football play because we got them out of field-goal range and they had to punt the ball away. I had a similar play in Super Bowl XXV when I sacked (Jim) Kelly to knock the Bills out of field-goal range. That's another play I'll never forget and I actually have a picture of that play as well.

The first sack came on third down and forced them to punt. The next one was the one that really broke their backs. The score was 16-14 at the time and they were trying to get back on top. We didn't let them and from there, we just took off. Phil Simms just started completing passes and we were able to run the football. By the start of the fourth quarter, all of our fans were going crazy. It was a wild scene.

How well we did on defense in that game was never really talked about all that much. All that was talked about was Phil, and you had to root for that. But Lawrence, Carl (Banks), and I just killed them in the run game.

If Phil Simms didn't have the day he did, I don't know who would have been the MVP. There might have been co-MVPs, Carl Banks and I, because both of us had a dominant game. But the win is the most important thing and we got it.

There are two times in life that you can never top if you're an athlete. The first is the birth of your first child. That came for me in 1995 when my daughter, Arianna Nicole, was born. The second is winning your first championship. You're fortunate enough to get to play a kid's game for a king's ransom and then to win a championship is an unbelievable feeling. Getting a chance to do that makes you wonder, "Where do you go from here?"

It was so much fun to do it with all the great guys I was able to. That '86 team was the closest team that I've ever been on. We all still stay in touch with and root for each other. To get a whole team to come together and love each other like that for a whole season is real cool.

That team should have won four Super Bowls. Ask Phil, he'll tell you the same thing. From 1986-91, maybe not '87, but every other year we should have either won the Super Bowl or been in position to win it. That's just how good a football team we had. We could have been as good as the '70s Steelers, '80s 49ers, or '90s Cowboys. The sad thing is that we never achieved that because of all the other stuff we had to overcome.

Another sad thing is that I don't think I or the entire defense as a whole got enough credit for how well we played in a 3-4 defense. To end up with (83.5) sacks in a career in a three-man line is just unheard of. Not even Lee Roy Selmon, who was probably the guy I patented my game around, had that type of success in a 3-4 defense.

People always ask me why I'm not in the Hall of Fame. Well, the Hall of Fame is all politics. It's not so much about who showed up and did what, how many championships they won, or how valuable they were to their team; it's just all about politics. There needs to be a better way to judge players based on productivity and ability to help teams win championships.

GAME RESULTS

Despite winning their first Super Bowl championship in a 39-20 rout, the Giants actually trailed at halftime, 10-9. However, the words of Broncos head coach Dan Reeves regarding the midpoint score said it all.

"That was about the best half of football we played all year, and when we were only ahead by a point, I didn't feel all that good about what the second half was going to bring," Reeves said.

As Marshall noted, one of the game's biggest plays came right before halftime with the Broncos on top 10-7. Right before intermission, George Martin dropped John Elway for a safety that totally swung the game's momentum.

In the second half, the Giants' offense got on track, as Phil Simms posted most of his 22-of-25, 268-yard, three-TD performance after the break.

A 17-point third quarter left New York in front, 26-10, and firmly in charge heading into the game's final 15 minutes.

Marshall was one of the key defenders who throttled Elway and Co. all game long. He sacked the Denver signal-caller twice, and he led the Giants defense with 17 postseason pressures and three sacks. He also topped the D-line with 11 tackles in the playoffs.

Chapter 10

BOBBY JOHNSON

THE YOUNG LIFE OF BOBBY JOHNSON

Like most professional athletes, Bobby Johnson excelled at multiple sports when he was growing up. In addition to being a solid student, Johnson shined at football, baseball, basketball, and track before choosing the gridiron, because "football was always a lot more exciting." However, not every starry-eyed 11-year-old has to deal with the divorce of his parents.

As a result, it looked like Johnson's single mother was not going to be able to send him to Assumption Catholic High School in East St. Louis, Illinois. That's when the school's football coach, James Monken, stepped in and provided Johnson the support that played a huge part in him reaching the NFL.

"He was great," Johnson stated. "He actually helped pay the tuition. I appreciate everything he's ever done for me."

In addition to his monetary help, Monken's support and guidance also helped Johnson along the way.

"I played quarterback in high school and my high school coach (Monken) kept telling me to get my grades and that I could go to school and continue to go further," he said. "He encouraged me to keep my mind into it and to keep my head straight."

Johnson took care of the rest.

THE GAMES OF MY LIFE
GIANTS VS. EAGLES—SEPTEMBER 2, 1984;
GIANTS AT VIKINGS—NOVEMBER 16, 1986
BY BOBBY JOHNSON

While the Minnesota game, and the fourth-and-17 catch, in 1986 was a very big game for me, I honestly think that my best game was my first ever game.

My first catch as an NFL receiver went for a touchdown against the Philadelphia Eagles when I was a rookie. I didn't think Phil (Simms) was actually going to throw me the ball, but I happened to be open and he threw it my way. I actually scored twice that day.

Before that game, I kind of just kept to myself. I was trying my best not to be too nervous or think too much. I had to make sure that I ran the right routes and didn't make any mistakes, like misreading a safety or corner blitz or anything like that. My focus was to make sure that I had all the plays down and to remember everything that I had to do.

I was so nervous. I was starting, but I didn't even think that I was going to catch a pass, let alone a touchdown. I caught the two touchdown passes and had 137 yards receiving. I was so happy I didn't know what to do.

After I scored that first touchdown, I really didn't know how to react. To this day, I still think I was dreaming the whole thing. I thought, "This cannot be happening to me on a Sunday afternoon in Giants Stadium." It was amazing.

It was my first true NFL game, and I had all these media members around me afterward. It was crazy. I had never seen that many reporters in my whole life. I didn't know what to say. There were cameras there and people firing questions my way; I didn't know what the heck I supposed to do. I was stuttering; I was in a state of shock. I was like a little kid in a candy shop. I was still amazed just to be able to play with Lawrence Taylor and Phil Simms. It took quite a while until I could actually comprehend and digest that I was really playing with these guys.

It was a blast, and it was incredible. I was so nervous during the game that I didn't even think to save either of the touchdown balls. I sure wish that I had, but obviously I wasn't expecting any of this to happen. I probably spiked them after I scored.

I didn't keep any press clippings or pictures from that game although I'd sure like to have them. I never saved anything from when I played but nowadays I wish that I did. You'd like to have that stuff to be able to look back at from time to time.

I know that I impressed Coach (Bill) Parcells a lot during training camp that summer. As a rookie free agent (from Kansas) in camp, I knew that it was going to be hard to make an impression on Coach Parcells, but I must have. Actually my first catch in the preseason was also a touchdown. It was all like a blur in a dream. It was happening, but I didn't know how to comprehend it at the time. I led the team in touchdowns (with seven) that season, my rookie year.

I think having a game like that right off the bat showed Parcells and the people of New York that they made the right choice in keeping me on the team coming out of training camp and gave them comfort knowing that they could throw me the ball in key situations. That helped quite a bit. I always just tried to catch everything that came my way.

During the '86 season two years later we were on a roll and always knew that we could make a play when we needed to. However, facing a fourth-and-17 in Minnesota with the game on the line made even us a little worried. If it was third down, we would have thought we could get it done in two plays, but needing that many yards on one play with the game hanging in the balance was a lot of pressure on all of us.

We had run a lot of those type routes and situations in practice so we were kind of prepared. To me, it was just like any other play. I was going to do my job and everyone else would do theirs, and then you just hope it works.

You honestly can't possibly be too confident before a play like that. You just have to hope that everything clicks at the same time. First of all, you need good protection. That's where it started, with the front line. They had to give Phil good protection. If he didn't have the time, none of that would have happened. Then, Ali (Haji-Sheikh) had to make the field goal, too.

From what I can recall the play call was 74/18 with some other options. My route was just a 20-yard comeback. I don't think my route called for me to go that long, but if you have any kind of football knowledge you know that you had better at least get to the first-down marker when it's fourth down.

I was Phil's third option on that play, but he told me in the huddle to keep my eyes on him and be ready because he might be throwing it my way. I just ran to the sticks toward the sideline and he threw it perfectly. I didn't do anything extraordinary on the play. Right after I caught it I wasn't even thinking what an enormous play I had just made. To me, at the time, it was just another play in the game to help us win.

We didn't lose another game after that. We got home-field advantage throughout the playoffs and all that good stuff. I listen to television announcers say that one play doesn't change a whole game or even a season. But if you look back through the years, there are definitely some plays in Giants history that have changed games and even seasons, and that play against the Vikings was definitely one of them. One play can definitely make a game. After that we believed in ourselves more so than ever. It does take a little luck to go on a run like that and go undefeated, but our confidence was so high after the Minnesota game that we all believed we were going to win it all. I didn't think anybody could beat us that year and we proved it.

The locker room after that game was crazy. We all got together and we knew we were going to go on a run. We knew anything was possible and that anything could happen. We couldn't say it out loud at the time, but we all knew that we had the best team.

I don't think the magnitude of that play and that game fully sunk in until the next day. You would think, "Did this actually happen?" right after it unfolds. As a football player growing up, all you're worried about is starting in high school. Then it's on to college. Even once you make the pros, you sure don't think that you're going to win the Super Bowl during your first three years.

I still get chills just thinking about it. I cried like a baby after we won the Super Bowl. I had my mother and father there. It doesn't get any better than that.

GAME RESULTS

The 1984 season opener marked the return of quarterback Phil Simms, who had missed basically the entire previous two seasons due to injury. His favorite target that day was rookie free agent Bobby Johnson, who tallied eight catches for 137 yards and a pair of scores. Simms connected with Johnson for a 35-yard touchdown that gave New York a

Justin Tuck takes down Tom Brady for a safety in
the first half of Super Bowl XLVI. | *AP Images*

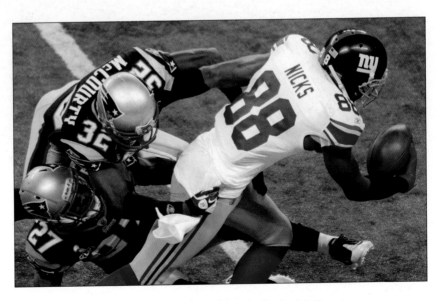

Hakeem Nicks charges through Devin McCourty
and Antwaun Molden. | *AP Images*

Victor Cruz weaves behind Jerod Mayo to catch a
two-yard touchdown pass. | *AP Images*

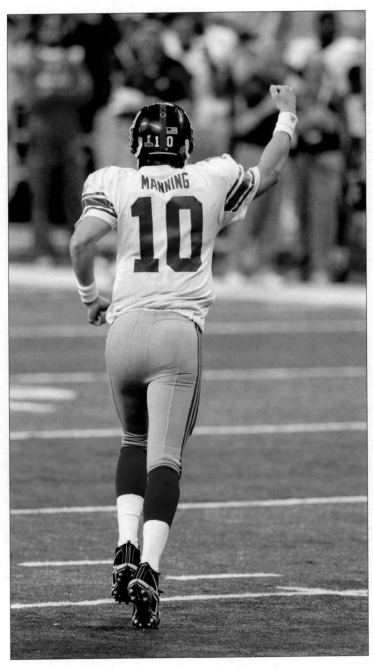

Eli Manning celebrates the first Giants touchdown
of Super Bowl XLVI. | *AP Images*

Ahmad Bradshaw and Eli Manning complete a seamless
handoff in the first half. | *AP Images*

Bradshaw once again demonstrates why he is one of the elite running backs in the NFL as he leaves Patriots safety Patrick Chung in the dust. | *AP Images*

Defensive end Jason Pierre-Paul celebrating on the field after dominating the Pats offense. | *AP Images*

Justin Tuck's third-quarter sack helped pave the
way to victory. | *AP Images*

To Bill Belichick's chagrin, Mario Manningham keeps both feet on the field as he makes a critical catch in the second half. | *AP Images*

Wide receivers Victor Cruz (left) and Hakeem Nicks (right) hoist the coveted Vince Lombardi trophy. | *AP Images*

Eli Manning and Tom Coughlin celebrating their second Super
Bowl victory over the New England Patriots. | *AP Images*

21-6 halftime lead over Philadelphia. After the Eagles sliced New York's advantage to just a point, Simms fired a 16-yard strike to Johnson for the game-winning score in a 28-27 victory. What most people forget about Johnson's tremendous first career contest was that he also had a 66-yard reception negated due to penalty. Needless to say, he was the star of the show.

"I can't even imagine how that must have felt," said former Giants receiver Stephen Baker, who joined Big Blue three years after Johnson's big debut. "I'm sure he must have been brimming with confidence. If you can score two touchdowns in your first game, it seems easy. But we all know it's not."

Nor is it easy to convert a fourth-and-17 on the road with only 1:12 to play—with an entire game on the line. Yet, that's what Johnson did when he collected Simms' pass and stepped out of bounds at the Minnesota 30-yard line for a 22-yard gain. That set up Raul Allegre's fifth field goal—a 33-yarder with 15 seconds remaining in the game—to give New York a miraculous 22-20 victory over the Vikings. Johnson also contributed a 25-yard TD catch and 22-yard end-around to New York's cause.

"Of course I was a fan at the time; I was still in college," Baker said. "But I remember that play very well. To make a catch like that has to be the best feeling. I've honestly never made a catch like that. I can't even put into words how that must have felt. I remember hearing the story about how the defensive line coach (Lamar Leachman) was standing on the bench, and when Bobby made that catch he fell down and almost broke his legs."

"That catch was arguably the most memorable play of that season," Giants President/CEO John Mara added. "I think we just all had the feeling after that game that this was going to be our year."

Eight wins later, New York had captured its first Super Bowl championship.

Chapter 11

AMANI TOOMER

THE YOUNG LIFE OF AMANI TOOMER

Amani Toomer's mother was reluctant to allow her son to play football, so Toomer took up soccer instead. That was until Toomer's father, Donald Sr., intervened. Giants fans couldn't be happier that he did.

"In sixth grade, my mom still didn't want me to play, but my dad snuck me off to football," Toomer recalled. "About halfway through the season my mom realized I wasn't playing soccer. That was the first organized football I ever played."

Toomer gives all the credit for his gridiron development to his father, who has worked the play clock at Raiders home games since the club moved back to Oakland in 1995.

"My dad had a key impact because he did the whole reverse psychology thing on me," Toomer said. "My dad wanted me to play football but then he'd say things like, 'That's okay, you're not tough enough. It's a tough sport. I don't know if you're tough enough.' I was like, 'Of course I'm tough enough.'"

Toomer was so tough that he began his football career as an offensive lineman.

"Right guard, number 63—a pulling guard," he laughed. "I was as fast as anyone on the team."

The following year, Toomer left the Berkeley Cougars and went to play for the rival Richmond Steelers, where they let him play running back.

"I went back and played my old team and we killed them," Toomer stated. "I remember they said they had a hit out on me and called me a traitor."

Toomer was still a running back at heart when he reached De LaSalle High School in Concord, California. Since the team was already littered with backs, Toomer was put at tight end and outside linebacker.

"I used to score on a play called 'Y Pop' all the time," he said. "It was a quick throw to the tight end and I'd just take off and run."

By spring practice of his sophomore year, Toomer was given his first chance to try out for varsity receiver.

"I remember going to school the next day and telling everyone and they all were like, 'Shut up, you're not even that good,'" he said. "I honestly had a tough time trying to learn how to play receiver. I really wasn't that good; I was dropping a lot of balls. But then I had one time during a summer practice game where I think I scored four touchdowns and ever since then I knew I belonged on varsity."

While Toomer scored on only the second catch of his high school career, his defining moment would come later that season. De LaSalle faced off for the league championship with Pinole Valley, where Toomer's older brother Donald was a senior cornerback.

"He was a corner so I was trying to kill him the whole game," Toomer said. "But he was throwing me around pretty good. They were ahead late, but I caught a kickoff, broke loose and ran up the sideline. He was trying to catch me. He grabbed my jersey but not enough to bring me down. I got free and dove into the end zone and the whole crowd went crazy. It was great.

"To this day, that was the biggest play of my life. We won the game and I outran my brother. He was dominating me the whole game, but when I finally got a chance to run with him he couldn't catch me. That was the best."

Amani Toomer is New York's all-time leading receiver.
John Cordes, Icon Images

THE GAME OF MY LIFE
GIANTS VS. JAGUARS—DECEMBER 23, 2000
BY AMANI TOOMER

It was the final game of the 2000 season and we were playing for home-field advantage. I had 900 (901) yards coming into that game, so I needed around 100 (99) for 1,000 on the season. I was fully expecting that I wasn't going to get the 1,000; I was resigned to the fact. But then I went into the game and they threw me the ball eight times. I caught all eight balls and ended up with 193 yards. The whole game I was totally focused.

It was funny because it ended up being a game that didn't really mean anything in terms of the big picture of us going to the Super Bowl. Two days later, the Vikings lost anyway, so we really didn't need to win that game. But it was just great because at the time—before the Vikings lost to Indianapolis—we were playing for so much. I think for you to have a great game it has to be for something big, something has to be on the line. Before we knew that Minnesota lost, this game was for home-field advantage throughout the playoffs. We were all pumped.

We were playing a Jacksonville team that didn't make the playoffs, but it wasn't too bad (the Jags finished 7-9). That's the game I remember the most. One of the plays that stood out to me is when I ran one route and the ball got tipped. I stopped, adjusted, and I was able to catch it. From that point on, I knew that was going to be a day where everything was going to fall my way. It came early in the game and it was a great sign of things to come. That game was special for me. I'll never forget that game.

I caught a long touchdown at the end of the game that went for 54 yards. That turned out to be my longest TD of the season. I remember the ball was thrown behind me, but I spun around and caught it and started running up the sidelines.

I felt different that afternoon. For some reason I didn't think I was going to get the ball enough to break the 1,000-yard mark. I figured we'd get caught up in running the ball and with all of our weapons that I'd get lost in the crowd. So I was kind of upset about that. When they threw me the ball I remember going after it as aggressively as possible and thinking, "You're not going to take this from me."

Usually during timeouts I'd sit down, but I was so excited that I was pacing the sidelines back and forth. That game I was extra focused, almost to the point where I wasn't even comfortable.

We were fighting the whole game. They went ahead at one point but then we came back for the win. We played really bad as a team early in the game, but suddenly we turned it on. And we carried that momentum all the way to the Super Bowl.

That had to be the biggest game I had played in during my career up to that point. We were never really that good. We only went to the playoffs once before then (in 1997) and we were in and out in one game. So this was a big game.

I always try to downplay things going into games. I was thinking to myself that if we lost, the second seed in the playoffs wouldn't be that bad. We would have one home game before an away game. I do that to calm myself down, but once I get into the game, that all changes. Once the game started, I was thinking we definitely had to win everything so we could be that top seed. That would make teams have to try to beat us in our stadium. At the time, we had a huge advantage at home because we had the grass tray field that only we really knew how to play on. Players on other teams would be slipping and sliding, but we had it down; we knew how to play on that field.

I remember their running back, Fred Taylor, popping off during the week about what he was going to do against our defense. That was kind of indicative of the whole season, because no one gave us our just due. Everyone was telling us we were the worst team to ever make the Super Bowl and stuff like that. So we kind of just took talk like that in stride. But at this point, we were about to clinch being the best team in the NFC and a team that wasn't even going to make the playoffs is going to come up here and tell us how bad we are? That definitely pissed a lot of us off. We knocked him out of the game—Shaun Williams nailed him a couple times and took him out. That goes to show how far that talking got them.

As the game went along, I really wasn't too sure how close I was to the 1,000-yard mark. It was in the back of my mind, but I wasn't sure. I had struggled earlier that year. At the midpoint of the year (after seven games) I only had like 300 (288) yards. Then I had three 100-yard games in the next four. When I got to 1,000 yards, it was a big deal to me. Even though I had started that season out shaky, which I normally don't do, I was able to regroup and finish out the year strong. Coming back from adversity is something that's always driven me.

I remember sitting on the sideline later in the game thinking, "Did I get it?" Ike Hilliard was right next to me, and he said, "C'mon, man, you know you got it." Sometimes when you're on the field you just get caught up in things. That's when you know you're having a good game when you're not thinking about how many catches you have or your stats. You really lose yourself out there and those are the games you love to play. When you're aware of everything going on, there's always going to be something holding you back.

That was only my second year starting so I still felt like people weren't really taking me seriously. Honestly, I still feel that way today—that I haven't gotten my just due. The first year I topped 1,000 yards, everyone said it was easy to do once. But after I did it the second year, that's when I really felt like I belonged in that upper echelon.

There are teams throughout your career that you really enjoy playing on and that Giants team was one of them. The 2002 team was another one like that. In 2000, I don't know if we were the best team I've ever played on as far as talent-wise, but we were a team that didn't make any mistakes and we made teams beat us. Most games in this league are lost instead of won and we almost never beat ourselves. That's why we were so successful.

Having the feeling that you know you're going to win every week is a different kind of feeling. It's a lot better than going out there thinking, "I hope everything turns out alright." It's really something that's so honest that you can't fake it. It's a feeling you get and an expectation you have. No matter what, you're not going to hit the panic button. We're going to compete, and if a team is going to beat us, they're really going to have to beat us, but it didn't happen that way very often.

Everyone on that club wanted to win so badly. We enjoyed each other, we enjoyed coming in here. It was like a big hangout. The coaches would tell us to go home but we'd stick around and watch film or go in the steam room. We were a really close team that really enjoyed playing together. When we got on the field, we really put it all together. I just remember really enjoying playing with that group of guys.

That season is mostly remembered for our coach, Jim Fassel, guaranteeing that we were going to make the playoffs. I just remember thinking, "Yeah, we're 7-4, of course we're going to the playoffs." I really figured we were going to the playoffs anyway. It wasn't a motivating factor to me.

I got hurt during the Eagles playoff game and that kind of messed up the whole Super Bowl run for me. I could barely do anything. I thought that by the Super Bowl my ankle would have gotten better, but it actually got worse.

I scored the last TD in the NFC Championship Game win over Minnesota. My big catch—a seven-yarder—made it 41-0. I didn't even know if I was going to play that whole week. I remember sitting in the training room and the trainers kept telling me I probably wasn't going to be able to play. But then (offensive coordinator) Sean Payton came in and said that I had better get ready for the game because we were planning to attack them and throw it up early and often because they had the worst secondary he had ever seen. At that, I hopped off the training room table and said, "You know what? It's not that bad." Once he said that it made me feel a lot better. It was touch and go because I couldn't even run that Friday before the game. But then I came out and caught a couple passes early and felt much better.

I can honestly say that I thought we were going to kill Minnesota. Robert Griffith was the only guy they had; he made every tackle. Their defense was really that bad. As for the Super Bowl…well, we don't really need to go into that, now, do we?

GAME RESULTS

For the second consecutive week, the Giants bounced back from a second-half deficit to win, this time securing home-field advantage throughout the NFC playoffs in the process. Big Blue's offense exploded in the second half to lead the Giants past the pesky Jaguars, 28-25, in front of 77,924 joyous Giants fans.

"This is a tremendous tribute to these players," head coach Jim Fassel told *The Giant Insider*. "The resolve that these guys have shown. This team is mentally tough right now."

The 12-4 Giants finished the season as the NFC's top team and on a five-game winning streak.

Amani Toomer had a career game, catching eight passes for 193 yards and a TD.

"He's turned into a big-play receiver and is becoming a valuable asset," quarterback Kerry Collins told *The Giant Insider*.

Toomer's 54-yard catch-and-run score gave New York a 21-10 lead with 3:05 to play.

"I heard them calling a 'shot play,' and I was so happy," Toomer told *The Giant Insider*. "I knew I was going to get that ball because I needed it."

Despite all of New York's second-half offensive fireworks, including Toomer's clutch TD, the hard-fought contest's exclamation point didn't come until CB Jason Sehorn returned the Jags' desperation onside kickoff attempt 38 yards for a TD to make the score 28-18. He then recovered Jacksonville's final onside kick as well.

"I thought my touchdown was going to be the play of the game and then Jason goes and returns that kick for a touchdown," Toomer said. "Everyone was all excited and I was kind of like, 'Alright, that's just how it goes.'"

Running back Tiki Barber also topped the 1,000-yard mark against Jacksonville. He stated that he was in very good company with Toomer.

"Not only is he a great teammate and a friend for life, in my mind, he is the most underrated receiver in the National Football League the past six or seven years," Barber said. "He has been nothing but productive and reliable for the Giants and he did it in a classy, unpretentious manner. Amani is one from the 'old school,' you could always expect him to give every ounce of himself every Sunday."

Chapter 12

RODNEY HAMPTON

THE YOUNG LIFE OF RODNEY HAMPTON

Could you imagine Rodney Hampton setting records as a member of the NBA's New York Knicks? Neither could any of Hampton's family and friends, who are the primary reason Hampton got his football career back on track. After ninth grade, Hampton decided to trade in the pigskin for the round ball. That didn't last long.

"I decided I was going to be a basketball star," Hampton laughed. "That was until my brother Randy, who did the same thing and quit playing football for basketball, as well as my father (Lee), my buddy Jarrett Scales and his father, J.B., who was my godfather, convinced me—no, I should say, made me—go back and play football."

Fortunately for Giants fans, Hampton listened. After missing one off-season, he was right back in action on the gridiron the following campaign.

"It was a short retirement after my ninth grade year," he said. "They made me go back on the field. They all told me I wasn't going to be tall enough to play basketball. I got tired of putting on all the pads, cleats, and the helmet. I thought I could just put on my shorts and sneakers and go play basketball.

"But then I realized my jump shot wasn't that deadly, and since I'm no 6-9 guy, I think I made the right decision. I thank those guys for being in my life and making me go back and play."

Hampton and his quartet of "advisors" still laugh about that decision to this day.

"It worked out well, you could say," he said.

But Hampton is still quick to point out that his return to football did nothing to diminish his hardwood skills at Houston's Kasmere High School.

"I still played basketball and made the varsity squad in 10th grade," Hampton added. "I was a guard. I was quick as a cat. All my points came on dunks and lay-ups."

THE GAME OF MY LIFE
GIANTS VS. VIKINGS—NFC WILD CARD,
JANUARY 9, 1994
BY RODNEY HAMPTON

I had a pretty good game against the Vikings in the playoffs, scoring two touchdowns and running for 161 yards. My long touchdown run in the second half pretty much won the game for us. There was a playoff atmosphere and we had to come from behind to win the game. This game was my best because we were home and we won. I had a game against the Cowboys (December 17, 1995) where I had more yards (187), but we lost the game at the last second. You want to have a good game, but you have to win in order for it to be fulfilling personally.

On my long touchdown run (51 yards) against the Vikings, I can still recall going through the line of scrimmage and stiff-arming a couple guys and getting into the end zone. It was a long run and I was able to stiff-arm a linebacker, and at the end a safety came up and I was able to stiff-arm him and get into the end zone.

That run was set up by a fourth-and-2 play that we converted. I was able to grind it out for the first down. I got hit by a linebacker but was able to spin out of it. I had to push off another hit and then I got the first down. That kept the momentum going and shortly after that, we hit them with the long touchdown run. That fourth-down play was probably as big as the touchdown run because that really got the crowd into it. The next thing you know, we had the long run. Then, our defense stuffed

One of running back Rodney Hampton's 33 carries during the game of his life against the Minnesota Vikings. *Bill Hickey, Getty Images*

them right up and we came back once more and I had a two-yard touchdown run that pretty much sealed the game.

That was a statement that Coach Dan Reeves had trust in our line and obviously he had trust in me. We needed momentum because we were pretty much dead at that point. It's funny that two yards can turn around the whole game and get everyone into it, but it certainly did in this game. It sparked us and it sparked the fans.

At halftime during that game we came in and we were down 10-3, but all the guys stayed calm. Our thought was, "Don't talk about it, be about it." All the talking wasn't going to do anything. Basically we knew we had to come out in the second half and make something happen; we still had 30 minutes left to play. We knew we had to win or go home.

Then we went out and got it done. I always appreciated my linemen, just like they appreciated me. We had a nice chemistry, and, as a team, we were known for running the ball. If we had the lead, other teams knew they were in trouble. We were always able to grind it out and run out the clock in the fourth quarter. That's the kind of team we had all year and we were able to do it again.

It was very important to us that we won that playoff game. We had played well all season, but if you don't win at least your first playoff game, it all really means nothing. You don't want to get hit with that tag—like Peyton Manning had before he finally won—that you can't win the big game. Once you get that off your back, you can be more relaxed going forward. It's important not to get too anxious just because it's a big game. If you approach it like it's just another game, you'll be relaxed and able to play like you had the whole season.

It was exciting since it was a playoff game, but I always approached every game the same. I had been playing football since I was little, so once you learn the fundamentals of the game, you just have to go do your job. There was no need to go and put extra pressure on yourself—just go out and have fun. Even though there'd be at least 70,000 people at Giants Stadium, you really could just block it out. Once you see it on TV after the game, you realize how exciting everything was. The Giants fans were rocking and rolling, as usual. But once you're on the football field you just learn to block all the outside stuff out.

My dad, Lee Hampton, was up for that game. It meant an awful lot having him there and knowing he was on hand to witness that game. It was good for me to have a good game in front of him and some of my friends. That made their trip that much more exciting and memorable. After the game, Coach Dan Reeves gave me the game ball and I still have it right in my trophy case.

I also remember one of the most memorable plays I ever had during my rookie year: My first ever carry in a Giants uniform. In the preseason against Buffalo, my first carry was a draw play. I got the ball on my own 11-yard line and I went 89 yards in Buffalo against the Bills. Everyone always remembers that Rodney's first carry went 89 yards for a touchdown. That helped me out a lot—entering the league and having success early. I was excited, mostly because I took advantage of an opportunity that presented itself to me. I could have slipped or fallen or made the wrong read and only gained a few yards. But I read my assignment, read my blocks, and hit everything full speed, just like I always did. Football's the same from little league all the way to the pro level. People just get bigger, faster, and stronger along the way.

I remember Coach Parcells always had you on your toes. After that run, he pulled me over and said, "Hey, you're not in Canton yet." He helped me to stay focused and made sure that I was prepared to play every week.

I felt real good about my entire Giants career. But I can honestly say that I knew it could have been better. Coming in from Georgia, no one really knew exactly how serious my knee injury was. I just feel blessed that I was able to play eight years. Having David Meggett around as our third-down back also helped me out because I didn't have to take the pounding I would have if I was the full-time guy. I stayed humble and just overcame the knee injury. I wasn't able to do a lot of things because of my knee, but I made it through my whole career without too many people knowing about it. I looked at myself as a back that could also catch the ball out of the backfield and could make people miss like I did in my early years. As the knee slowed me up, I gained more weight, but then I was able to use that to become a more powerful between-the-tackles runner with good vision to make people miss.

If it wasn't for the knee, I think I would have been a guy who was able to put up numbers like Marshall Faulk. I could have been the kind of guy who could do basically anything on the football field. But overall, I had a great career and I wouldn't take anything back.

While my knee bothered me my whole career, no one really knew about that. If you look at it, I missed a couple games almost every year because of my knee. I just kept my mouth closed and did my best each week. I never had more than 1,200 yards in a season but I ended up with close to 7,000 yards for my career and that was with me missing a couple games every year. You wonder what I could have come up with if I had played full seasons. But I can say that now; I couldn't say that back then. It wouldn't have been too smart to say anything back then. But I always tell people that I was glad that I was able to play eight years even without having the full service and cutting ability of my knee. It worked out that we turned into a grind-it-out football team where I was able to use my strength, size, vision, and ability to lean forward and get the tough yardage to be an effective running back for the New York Giants.

GAME RESULTS

As expected, the Giants Stadium winds were whipping in early January. The Giants won the coin toss and elected to take the wind instead of the ball. It translated into a 26-yard David Treadwell field goal that broke the ice. However, the Vikings took better advantage of their wind-aided opportunities in the second period. Minnesota scored on a 40-yard Jim McMahon-to-Cris Carter TD and a 52-yard Fuad Reveiz field goal to take a 10-3 lead into the locker room at halftime.

As Rodney Hampton explained, there was no panic or concern on New York's part following the first 30 minutes of action. The game's third quarter belonged to Hampton, who scored on runs of 51 and two yards to give the Giants a 17-10 lead they would not relinquish.

Minnesota only came close to tying the game once after Hampton's outburst, but Myron Guyton poked the ball free from Carter and Greg Jackson recovered at the New York 15-yard line to squash the threat.

All told, Hampton finished the game with franchise record-tying marks of 33 carries and 161 yards. Rob Carpenter exploded for the same impressive numbers on December 27, 1981 in Philadelphia. Hampton also chipped in with six receptions for 24 yards.

Chapter 13

JESSIE ARMSTEAD

THE YOUNG LIFE OF JESSIE ARMSTEAD

Imagine growing up in Dallas and overshadowing the beloved Cowboys—while you're still in high school, no less. Welcome to Jessie Armstead's world.

Before his freshman season, Armstead didn't even have a position. By his sophomore campaign, he was already being touted by *USA Today* as one of the nation's top high school football players.

Armstead selected the linebacker position he played so successfully solely because he was the same size as his best friend.

"We went down the line and the coach asked you to stand up and say what position you play," Armstead recalled. "I had no idea what to say, but my best friend said linebacker, and I was about his size so I said linebacker too."

Talk about a quick learner.

"I was just raw when I first started playing," Armstead said. "I did all that just playing naturally. You could only imagine what was going to happen when I had a little more knowledge of the game."

Yes, you could. By the time he left Carter High School, Armstead was the main cog in the school's Class 5A state championship team, having racked up 302 tackles, nine sacks, and five interceptions along the way.

With it, however, came more attention than most high school players are accustomed to.

"It helped me in the long run," he said. "Not too many people growing up in Texas can ever say that people would rather see you than the Cowboys. I know there were instances in restaurants where people would come to see me even before they'd go to those guys.

"I experienced it all at a young age. So I wasn't overwhelmed when I got to college, and then when I got to the pros as far as publicity and all that. I had already been there. I had been on the top of the mountain before."

Armstead credits his persistent, hard-working mom and honest, intelligent father for helping him realize his potential.

But he wouldn't remain on top forever. A torn ACL suffered during his senior year resulted in a drop to the eighth and final round of the 1993 NFL Draft, when the Giants mercifully selected him. But even then, Armstead knew he belonged.

"I was as low as I could go when I got drafted in the last round," he said. "At that time, I knew that none of the guys that went before me were better than me. I knew that then and history has shown it to be true.

"I was born to play football. I knew where I was headed."

THE GAME OF MY LIFE
GIANTS VS. COWBOYS—OCTOBER 5, 1997
BY JESSIE ARMSTEAD

There are only so many tackles you can make in a pro game. We played Dallas and I had 18 tackles. It was a great game for me; if you can come up with that many, you've obviously done something right. It seems like you've controlled the whole game by yourself.

It was a home game in 1997 and we beat them (20-17). It just seemed like no one could stop me no matter what they did. I've felt like that many times during my career, but this time it really just seemed like it was so much easier. I didn't have to work as hard as I normally do out there. You always get in that zone where you can see things and feel things, but sometimes you get into that special zone where everything you think is going to happen, happens exactly how you think it will.

Jessie Armstead went to five Pro Bowls playing linebacker for the Giants.
Ed Nessen, Icon Images

I remember making a lot of big hits that day, hitting Emmitt (Smith) a lot, and making a lot of plays. Any time you put that many on the ground, you know you've had a big day.

All throughout the game, my teammates were joking with me and telling me to save some tackles for them. Guys in the secondary were coming up to me in the huddle saying, "Save me a tackle, man, you're making all the tackles." That makes you feel good, because you know the guys behind you don't have to worry about making any big stops that day.

I've always said that if I get the first two tackles of the game, it's on. I'm ready to go and I'm coming for you. You know by the end of the first series what kind of game it's going to be. And I knew very early in that game that no one was going to want to mess with me that day.

I had a lot of big games and big plays during my career, but it always meant more to me if it came against Dallas. There was always something about those Dallas games for me personally. You're always looking for that one little edge to push you over during games, but against them not only did I have that edge, I had a big chip.

I loved New York, but as a kid you always dreamed of playing for your hometown team. After they passed on me in the draft I kind of felt like I got kicked out of town. That was my attitude: that I got kicked out of Texas. That's why I always played with a chip when we faced them. Without a doubt, beating them was more special to me than beating any other team.

I still have the game ball from that game; I kept most of them. The first game ball I ever got came in 1995 when we beat Arizona in overtime. I had the game-winning interception return to end it. That was right when I first came in and that play broke me right into the league. That was a big game right there.

At the time, I wasn't a starter yet, but I played a lot. At the end of regulation all the coaches were talking about how we needed someone to step up and make a play. We were on defense first and all they wanted us to do was stop them and then hope our offense could drive for a field goal. But my mind was thinking something else. I got my hands on the ball and returned it all the way, 58 yards, and we won the game. I was so excited that I didn't even realize we had won the game right there on that play. I was getting ready to line up for the extra point before I realized it was all over and I had won it. I also got the special teams game ball for that one. I put in a full day's work on two sides of the ball.

That was one of the biggest plays and one of my biggest highlights because it was still the start of my career and everyone was watching to see if I could make plays. After that, I convinced them that I had to be a starter.

Walking off the field after both of those games, I thought to myself that I couldn't wait until next week. You get on such a high after a win like that and you don't want to stop; you'd be ready to go right back out there if they'd let you. I was very thankful that everything that happened did, but you can't wait until next week because you want to show people more.

I always believed in being consistent. If you looked at my whole career, I never really had any slumps. I might be one of the only players ever to play more than 10 years and never have a slump. I played from my heart. The only way that I'd ever have a slump is if my heart went away. When that happens it's time for you to walk away.

Everyone in the National Football League has talent, but if you don't have a big heart, you won't get anywhere. Talent is overrated. You can put two guys out there with the same talent level and the one with the bigger heart is going to win every time. I always just wanted it more. You have to refuse to lose.

That was especially easy against Dallas. It was extra sweet having a huge-tackle game like that against the Cowboys. It's always been that you have to get after the Cowboys because they're one of our biggest rivals. But personally I've had it out for Dallas forever. One of my favorite stories is that Jimmy (Johnson) had a chance to draft me and he made a big mistake at the time by listening to the University of Miami coaching staff. We talked about it afterward and he said that he never listened to anybody else, but he finally did and passed over on drafting me. I've always carried that chip after that.

Jimmy admitted that if he had done all the thinking himself he would have made a better decision and drafted me. He told me before the draft that if I was still there in the sixth round he was going to get me. But he made a last-minute call to Miami and they didn't sound too positive about me so he backed off. Then I fell all the way to the eighth round, which doesn't even exist anymore.

All it would have taken to draft me was a little common sense. All the numbers and talk involved in the draft are overrated anyway. All you had to do was look at it and follow my history to see how I progressed from winning a championship at junior high school and being the star of the team. Then I went to the toughest high school in Texas football and became the top player in the nation for three years. After that I went to Miami, played in every game as a freshman and won a national championship there. I think that should show you right there what I was capable of. I don't know what their thinking was. They just got too smart and forgot that it just comes down to basic football and life.

But I think by now everyone has realized that I could play a little football. I enjoyed my entire Giants career a great deal. I think it was one of the best careers a player can have considering all the battles I had to fight to get the starting job. There were a lot of times I knew I should have been the starter and they knew I should have been the starter, but it was just how things worked out.

I was just blessed with an opportunity. When I came here I had every name-brand linebacker in front of me: Lawrence Taylor, Michael Brooks, Carlton Bailey, Steve DeOssie, and Corey Miller. These were guys I was looking to get autographs from, not beat out for a roster spot. That makes you feel even better knowing that the odds were stacked against you, yet you were able to come out on top.

I'll never forget the first time I met LT. During my high school career, *USA Today* had me ranked as the number-one linebacker in the nation so I was always being called "the next LT." When I finally met him in person, it was definitely a great feeling. He came to me after practice one day during my rookie year and said, "Man, you remind me of myself. I've never seen anyone run like that." That really boosted me up. Then he told the newspapers that so many people have been compared to him, but I was the closest to anyone like him that he had ever seen. That was a huge inspiration right there to keep pushing.

I found out years later from Phil Simms that the Giants had planned to cut me following our fourth preseason game that year in Miami. There were already designs for me to be released, but I played so well that they couldn't. Phil said he didn't want to tell me that until I was established, so he waited three or four years. It was basically predetermined that I was going to be out the door, but God blessed me and my talent helped me. I never realized that I was that close to being gone. Phil told me how proud he was of me, which meant a lot.

GAME RESULTS

New York had been battered and bruised by the 'Boys in the first meeting of the previous four seasons. But on this Sunday afternoon at Giants Stadium, Jessie Armstead wouldn't let them lose again. While Dallas marched up and down the field all game long, outgaining the Giants in total yards, 428-166, Armstead and his 18 tackles helped hold Dallas to only 17 points and the Giants were able to emerge victorious. Number 98 helped limit Dallas to only one touchdown on its five trips inside New York's red zone.

Armstead, who posted a dozen solo stops, was all over the field from the opening whistle. His presence no doubt forced Troy Aikman into some questionable throws—two of which were intercepted by Tito Wooten, including one he picked off in front of Michael Irvin and returned 61 yards for a touchdown late in the third quarter. That gave Big Blue a 13-9 lead they wouldn't relinquish. Before Wooten's heroics in the defensive showdown, Dallas had built a 9-6 lead on three Richie Cunningham field goals to Brad Daluiso's two.

New York survived a late Dallas threat, scoring on fullback Charles Way's three-yard TD run, and the playoff-bound Giants had evened their record at 3-3.

Former Giants GM Ernie Accorsi recalled Armstead's incredible play—not only that afternoon, but throughout his entire Giants career.

"Jessie Armstead will go down as one of my favorite players and favorite people of my career," Accorsi said. "They drafted him as a nickel linebacker and tried to slot him there because they thought at first he was going to be too small to be a full-time linebacker. But he became one and became an All-Pro."

Accorsi also noted that Armstead's worth extended well beyond his own stats.

"The greatest thing about Jessie was his leadership," he said. "He was the heart and soul of our defense."

Needless to say, when Jessie talked, the Giants listened.

"I remember coming back from Philadelphia on the bus after a big win, it was a game in which Jessie made a spectacular interception and returned it for a touchdown," Accorsi said. "One of our young players was playing music very loudly without ear phones and other players were getting annoyed but wouldn't say anything. Armstead got up and said,

'Turn that thing off or we're going to stop the bus and you're getting off.' The player turned it off."

Chapter 14

BRAD VAN PELT

THE YOUNG LIFE OF BRAD VAN PELT

Brad Van Pelt always wanted to be a part of the Michigan State family. He just wasn't sure that they wanted him back. Growing up 30 miles away from East Lansing, the Spartans were the obvious dream school of any athletic youngster. Almost 40 years later, it's Van Pelt who turned out to be a dream for the university. His tremendous four-year career at MSU was officially capped when Van Pelt was inducted into the College Football Hall of Fame in 2001.

"By the time I was eight or nine years old I started to play and follow football," Van Pelt recalled. "Having a major university that close made it easy. Those days Michigan State was a powerhouse, so I followed them. I grew up green and white and was fortunate enough to go there and play under Duffy Dougherty.

"But to tell you the truth, I lacked self-confidence. I think that lack of confidence actually helped me. I never thought that I was good enough to play at Michigan State. I thought I'd have to go elsewhere to have an opportunity to play."

That's when his brother, Robin, stepped in.

"My older brother wouldn't hear anything of it," Van Pelt explained. "He said it's a lot easier to step down than to step up. I went to Michigan State, everything worked out, and the rest is history. But to say I really thought I'd play there growing up wouldn't be true. I might have dreamt about playing there, but I never really actually thought that I would."

And boy, did he ever play there—as a three-sport star, no less. He captured the Maxwell Award, which signified the nation's best collegiate football player in 1972, and was MSU's Most Valuable Player that season as well. Additionally, Van Pelt was a two-time All-American and was thrice named All-Big Ten. He picked off 14 passes for the Spartans and returned two of them for touchdowns.

But that wasn't it. He also excelled in basketball and in baseball, enough so that the St. Louis Cardinals offered him $100,000 in bonus money.

"I ended up playing all three sports [at Michigan State]," Van Pelt said. "I went there on a football scholarship but was able to play the other sports, which is pretty much unheard of now because they want you to focus on your one sport. If they're paying your way, they want your time."

Van Pelt thoroughly enjoyed his time in northern Michigan.

"By far, I look back and say they were the four greatest years of my life," he said. "I was playing three major sports at a major college level. I was having fun and I met a great bunch of guys that I still stay in touch with.

"If I would have known how much fun I was going to have there, I would have gone to summer school."

THE GAME OF MY LIFE
GIANTS VS. LIONS—DECEMBER 5, 1976
BY BRAD VAN PELT

My dad passed away and we ended up playing Detroit a few weeks later. I don't remember the exact stats, but I had a really good game. It was in 1976 and it was an emotional game, because I had all my family members and friends present. It was just really emotional having everyone there under the circumstances, and I ended up having one of my better games.

During training camp that season is when my dad passed away. I basically flew home for the funeral, and then turned around and had to

Linebacker Brad Van Pelt came out of Michigan State and played 11 seasons for the Giants. *Robert Riger, Getty Images*

fly right back and suit up for a preseason game. It was kind of a weird situation for me.

My dad died from a heart attack, which was his second; he had another one late in the previous year. I had gone down to Florida with my mother and father while he was recuperating from the first one. He had lost a lot of weight and everyone thought he was in great shape. He was on this walking program one day, but judging by how far ahead he was of my mother, who was going to meet up with him, he must have started to jog or run. Then he had a massive heart attack and that was it.

I was very close with my father. He was a real role model to me. Knowing that he would have been sitting front and center for that game and wasn't able to obviously made it tough for me that afternoon. It was a game where I knew he was there, even though he wasn't sitting in the stands. Looking back, he's someone who I would love to have been more like.

I must have had at least 25 or 30 immediate family members and friends there, and then there were a couple busloads of people who had made the trip from my hometown. I can remember that tickets weren't too easy to come by for me that game. Fortunately, my teammates came through and I was able to collect enough for everyone to come.

It was on my mind for probably three weeks prior to the game that I wanted to have an outstanding game. I felt like I was in a different gear that day. It was a tremendous feeling just to play well in front of family and friends. My family used to travel to all the games, so not having him next to my mother was different and strange, but it was a great feeling to have such a great game.

I had a whole bunch of tackles (10). I know I had at least one sack (two, actually), and I think I even had an interception (again, two of them). That game really has always stuck out in my mind. Leading up to it and then going out and having that good of a game will always be special to me. I'm sure I've had better statistical games, but emotionally it was the best, for sure.

As charged up as I was for the game, I still just went about my business on the field. When I played, if I was fortunate enough to get a sack or make a tackle behind the line of scrimmage, I wasn't the rah-rah guy who went around beating my chest like you see nowadays. I just kind of went back to the huddle. That was my job and I just did it. As excited as I was, I don't remember doing anything differently out there on the field. And I certainly wouldn't have done it that day. I was just kind of in my own little world. By halftime I knew I was having a great game, but I was just focused on going out and continuing it in the second half.

I was able to spend some good time with the rest of my family after that game. It was a great weekend and a great homecoming of sorts. It was really everything that I hoped it would be. The fact that we won the game made it even better. But to be honest, whether we had won or lost, it was just important for me to have a good game.

Before the season Eddie Wagner, the equipment manager, had sewn a black armband onto my jersey to show that I had dedicated that season to my father. Back then, you could get away with stuff like that. The league office wasn't going to come down on you because your uniform wasn't to exact standards. Just the armband alone and me having to leave training camp made all of my teammates aware of what had happened without me even having to say anything to anybody. Then the fact that I was playing against my hometown team made just about everyone aware of it. I remember after the game it was a happy locker room and all my teammates were happy for me. It was a great feeling.

Back in those days we didn't win very often, so as much as I had personal motivation for this game, I also needed to make sure that we held the lead and won the game.

I still have a ball from that game, but I honestly don't know exactly where it is. I know I have it somewhere and I don't remember if it was a game ball or one of the interception balls that I always saved. I'm pretty sure it was given to me by the team. Either way, it's nice knowing that I have a keepsake from that game.

I think it was, by far, the most emotional game I've ever played in. I still get emotional talking about it to this day. Another cool part of the game is that there was a play where I had a sack and a forced fumble that's in my personal highlight tape. I came up on the quarterback (Greg Landry) and knocked the ball out of his hand. His arm was just starting to come forward when I knocked the ball away. That one play from that game I still have on film and can always see.

When I retired the Giants had a dinner for me and roasted me pretty good. They had coaches like Bill Belichick and Marty Schottenheimer getting on me. But the video crew put together a nice highlight tape of a lot of my plays and that big sack and forced fumble is on it. I'll bring it out whenever anyone wants to see me in action from the old days. It was nicely done by them and it's a great keepsake.

There was only one other moment in my entire career that I can look back on and remember so fondly. I still clearly remember with such enjoyment my first ever game that I was introduced with the starting lineup at Giants Stadium. I actually had goose bumps going up my arms when I ran out of the tunnel. Just hearing your name being announced and knowing that you had finally made it was phenomenal; knowing that your dream had come true.

Those are two of the greatest moments of my life, without a doubt.

GAME RESULTS

Brad Van Pelt would not let the Giants lose to Detroit, his hometown team, especially not with him having dedicated the game to his recently deceased father. Arnold Van Pelt died suddenly of a heart attack a few months before the contest at only 49 years old and this was the best way Van Pelt knew how to honor his dad. So Van Pelt went out and pretty much did it all on his own. He was named the NFL's Player of the Week after a 10-tackle, two-interception, two-sack outing as he led the Giants to a 24-10 victory over the Lions.

New York broke onto the scoreboard first when Ed Marshall caught an 11-yard touchdown pass from Craig Morton, and then extended it to a 10-0 lead on a 35-yard field goal by Joe Danelo. Doug Kotar's three-yard run offset a Detroit touchdown and field goal, and the Giants took a 17-10 lead into the locker room at halftime.

New York tacked on an insurance TD in the third quarter when Marshall and Morton hooked up once again, this time from 35 yards, to forge the game's final score, 24-10.

Harry Carson (11 tackles), Troy Archer (seven tackles and a sack), and John Mendenhall (five tackles, two sacks) aided Van Pelt's phenomenal defensive performance.

Van Pelt was riding high after being a key cog to victory in the most important game of his life. But Giants President/CEO John Mara recalled Van Pelt having to survive some rough times years earlier when he first joined New York.

"Brad was not very well received by the veterans in his rookie year," Mara said. "We were in a bidding contest with a baseball team (St. Louis) and we ended up signing him to what at the time was a very big contract. He was resented by many of the players because of that contract and all the attention he received. I can remember him at training camp sitting with the ball boys (including me) in the cafeteria rather than the players. In time he earned their respect with his play on the field and he became one of our most popular players in and outside the locker room."

Van Pelt was a member of New York's famed "Crunch Bunch" crop of linebackers. He joined Hall of Famers Lawrence Taylor, Harry Carson, and his very close buddy Brian Kelley to form one of the game's most feared and revered group of linebackers. All in all, the '70s were good times for Van Pelt, who was named the player of the decade by the Giants.

"He was a very good player on some bad teams," Mara said. "It was a shame that he was not around to share in the success we had in the mid-'80s."

Chapter 15

MICHAEL STRAHAN

THE YOUNG LIFE OF MICHAEL STRAHAN

Like father, like son. Michael Strahan credits his father, Gene, for all his successes. Gene Strahan served in the U.S. Army and was stationed in Mannheim, Germany, while Michael was growing up.

"My dad had a huge impact on my life and he still does," the younger Strahan said. "He was the most positive person as far as my career. He would always say, '*When* you make the league,' not '*If* you make the league.'"

Strahan said he couldn't have done anything without the help and support of his father.

"He was and still is always very positive about everything," Strahan said. "He's my biggest cheerleader and my biggest supporter. He's my guy. I couldn't have a better father than what I have. I was dealt a good hand."

Strahan has countless memories of his youthful days as an Army brat in Fort Bragg, North Carolina, where his father was a member of the 82nd Airborne Division.

"I remember waking up early in the morning with my dad and jogging with his platoon," Strahan said. "If you finished you got a big thing of your own Gatorade. Back in the '80s and '90s, having your own bottle of Gatorade was a real big thing. I remember back in 1978, '79, and '80 running with him. I was only seven or eight years old."

Those were life lessons Strahan still carries to this day.

"It just taught you that there's no quitting," he said. "When you see soldiers out there and these guys are training and you see their commitment; watching those guys and their commitment to everything was impressive.

"It's like me with football, nowadays. I'm committed to everything. I'm not here to go halfway. I'm not in it to be mediocre. I realize that I can last a long time in this league if I just want to be a mediocre player. But it's not in my genetic makeup to be mediocre. If I'm going to do it, I have to try to be the best at it, no matter what."

On the gridiron, he's clearly succeeded.

THE GAME OF MY LIFE
GIANTS AT CARDINALS—DECEMBER 6, 1998
BY MICHAEL STRAHAN

The best game that I ever had was in 1998 when we played the Arizona Cardinals in Arizona. We had just got beat by the 49ers in San Francisco on a Monday night the week before, so we just stayed out there. I don't know what it was, but the first half was the coldest game I've ever played. And it probably felt that way because we weren't really expecting cold weather and the team wasn't prepared for it at all. I remember everyone on the sideline asking (equipment manager) Eddie Wagner for jackets. He was like, "It's Arizona. We didn't bring any jackets." But by the second half of the game it was back to the typical Arizona heat. It was so unusual that it was so cold and so hot in one game.

I don't know what it was about that game, but I couldn't do anything wrong. I made every play I was supposed to make; I made plays I wasn't supposed to make. I read every offensive call. It was as close to me playing a perfect game as I've ever felt as far as physically being dominant and making things happen without even thinking about it. Every movement and every thought I had, none of them were wasted. Everything was positive; everything just worked.

I don't even remember my stats. I'm sure I had a sack or something. I'm sure I had some tackles, but I know that I was all over the field. I felt like I was gliding.

Michael Strahan set an NFL record with 22.5 sacks during the 2001 season. *Rich Kane, Icon Images*

I remember that I was extra focused for that game. We had just lost the week before. Maybe it was because we stayed out there and we had a week to be somewhere different. It gave us a chance to relax a little bit and take it all in. I decided right then and there that from this point on, I was just going to enjoy the game. I was having a good personal season at that point—I think I already had about 10 sacks—but I was feeling down about our season as a team.

I decided at that point to enjoy the game for what it is. It's a great game—so just love the game. That was the first game of my career that I just said, "Love it and enjoy it." Ever since that game I've been playing at this very high level that I still compete at today. That's definitely the one turning point in my career, that one game.

I just tried to be more positive during that game. I realized that whatever you do out there on the field, only you do it. You control everything. I control my attitude going into the game and when I was out there. I controlled my attitude toward everything about the game and how I was going to play. It was like complete empowerment over my attitude toward the game. That's sometimes hard to do because one of the biggest things players deal with is self-doubt. In this instance, for the first time ever, there was none of that. It was completely, "I know I'm going to do it," not, "I hope I can." That was a great feeling.

After we lost to the 49ers I was really down and felt like I was playing like garbage, even though I played very well that game and had two sacks. I was making myself feel like I wasn't a good player and that wasn't even true. I had my first Pro Bowl season (in 1997) and still felt bad about it. I wondered why I felt bad about it and I didn't know.

All of a sudden, everything made sense to me. I finally realized that I control every positive thought and every negative thought, and I just wiped all the negative ones away. That was my ultimate game. God, I felt good.

When I look back on that game, I think I definitely should have come to that realization sooner. Why wasn't I more positive before? Why didn't I know what I could do instead of going into the game hoping I could do something? Now when I go into games, I know I can do something; I know what I can do and I believe in what I can do. Before that point I was kind of hoping and wishing good things would happen. It was a turning point for my career.

Walking off the field after that game, I felt that everything was going to be good. I had just seen how being positive was going to bring good results. From that second on, I played well and pretty much performed at the level I expected I could play week-in and week-out. I've done as well as I could've ever thought possible. It finally sank in that I can control my own game more so than anyone else controlling it. My opponent doesn't control my game. Whatever they're trying to accomplish against me doesn't affect how I play. I truly am the only one who decides how well I play. And, like I said, that all depends on my attitude. That game changed my attitude from then on for the rest of my career.

One of my close friends called me after the game and said he thought that was the greatest game that I had ever played. That was a huge compliment coming from someone who watches every game. That meant an awful lot to me for him to say that. But I already recognized that because I had made up my mind to be positive.

I was making tackles and running down plays that I normally didn't do. In the past it wouldn't have happened because I would have thought too much to do it. I remember one play down by the goal line where (Cardinals quarterback) Jake (Plummer) faked the option and tried to pop pass it. I hit Jake before he even got the option out of his hand.

I just knew everything. Everything I thought about was right, every move I made was right. It basically showed me how powerful the mind is. We all know how powerful the mind is when you're injured and your mind blocks the pain—and when you're on the field and you stick your hand down to rush and you don't hear the crowd until the play is over. You understand how powerful your mind is when you want to block things out so that you can do what you need to do to accomplish something else. But in this case it was as if I tapped into another side of that which I had never touched before. That was just a side of complete positive thinking on the part of how I was going to play, what I expected of myself and even what I knew I was going to do, not what I hoped I was going to do.

I'm telling you, it makes the biggest difference in the world. From that moment on, when I go into a game, I know what I'm going to do. I don't worry about the guy blocking me. I think just the opposite. He's more worried about what I'm going to do to him than I am about what he's going to do to me. I have to play my game. I used to try to adapt my game to the offensive lineman and try to figure out what he does and does not do well, and in some instances you still have to do that. But for the most part, I think I know what I do well. Let him worry about stopping what I do well. Let me do it to the best of my ability and see if he can stop it. I've been fortunate enough that in a lot of cases they haven't been able to. I'm going to keep that same approach.

You totally feel like you're playing faster with that mind-set. And it started in that Cardinals game. Your hand's down, you're getting off when that ball is barely moving, and you're gone. You're not even looking at the ball, to be honest. You just feel it. It's almost like an outer-body experience in a way. Like somebody has a joystick and they've gone through a certain phase in a video game hundreds of times and they know which motion to use and where it'll take you. That's exactly what that game was like. It was almost like I was being guided by somebody outside of myself.

One of the best parts of that game was that it was obvious that everybody noticed. My buddy called, and the coaches gave me the game ball. It was even more special because everybody noticed what I had done. I realized that it was a turning point for me, but I didn't realize that everyone would notice how well I played that week and that's a great feeling.

I'm very thankful that I had that game. I tried a new mental approach and it obviously worked. It all changed from, "Can I?" and, "What if?" to, "When I," and, "I will." It taught me that if you expect things on the field, you will make them happen on the field. It even taught me that if you expect things off the field, they'll happen off the field. It taught me to be positive about all aspects of life. You can get and do anything, as long as you set your mind to it and believe it.

GAME RESULTS

The Giants rebounded from a crushing 31-7 loss in San Francisco by edging the Cardinals in Arizona, 23-19, six days later. To avoid two cross-country trips in less than a week, coach Jim Fassel decided to have his club remain out west to practice between games. As Michael Strahan suggested, perhaps the change of scenery did the Giants good.

The game at Sun Devil Stadium started in 39-degree weather, hardly what New York was expecting. On offense, an 87-yard scoring hook-up between quarterback Kent Graham and running back Tiki Barber, 124 rushing yards from Gary Brown, and a trio of Brad Daluiso field goals were basically all the Giants would need.

Fullback Charles Way bulled in from eight yards out late in the third quarter, giving New York a 20-17 lead and erasing all of a 17-7 deficit. But the Cards wouldn't go away quietly. Jake Plummer completed passes of 19 and 38 yards to move Arizona to the Giants' one-yard line. That's precisely when the Strahan-led defense took matters into its own hands.

Strahan and middle linebacker Corey Widmer dropped Arizona running back Mario Bates for a one-yard loss on first down. Then, in the play Strahan previously described, he knifed through the line and nailed Plummer for a two-yard loss. Cornerback Jeremy Lincoln capped the defensive stand with an end-zone interception on third down. A Daluiso field goal and an intentional safety by Giants punter Brad Maynard forged the final score.

On two other occasions, Strahan dropped ball-carriers for losses— Larry Centers for a three-yard loss late in the second quarter and Adrian Murrell for a loss of one yard in the fourth.

Strahan's final numbers in that contest didn't even come close to doing justice to the disruptive force he was in Arizona. He finished with a team-high seven tackles, a five-yard sack, and a forced fumble.

Ernie Accorsi was in his first year as Giants general manager in 1998.

"Strahan is a great player," he said. "He does two things as well as anyone I have ever seen in a pass-rusher: playing with leverage and playing the run. I'm not sure I have ever seen a great pass-rusher play the run any better than Michael Strahan."

Justin Tuck had the good fortune of being able to play behind Strahan for a few seasons. While he wasn't around for that classic Cardinals match, he recalls another time Strahan manhandled Arizona in 2005.

"The first time I really saw that Michael Strahan was really Michael Strahan was my rookie year against the Arizona Cardinals on opening day," Tuck said. "In preseason, he really didn't do a whole lot. But that first game against the Cardinals I saw him make one of the best plays I've ever seen a defensive end make. He didn't go around or underneath the offensive tackle; he went through him. He bounced off the offensive tackle on the ground and still sacked the quarterback. You just don't see people make plays like that in this league too often. You can tell he's been truly blessed to have that unique talent."

Tuck believes that throughout NFL history Strahan has no equal.

"He's probably the best defensive end that ever played," Tuck said. "He's been so consistent for so long, no matter what the offenses throw at him. I've seen him beat three people on one play and I'm not talking about three tight ends. I'm talking about a guard, a tackle, and a tight end all on the same play. He's done that consistently. To do that, you have to be considered one of the best ever."

According to Tuck, another of Strahan's impressive traits is the fear he puts into his opponents.

"Not only do his stats show it, but you can just see how opposing offenses react to him when he steps on the field, the respect level they have for him is huge," Tuck said. "Every game you have the line sliding to him, backs chipping him, tight ends staying in when they would normally go out. The respect other people have for him as a pass-rusher, a run-stopper, and as a complete defensive end is remarkable."

Chapter 16

PAT SUMMERALL

THE YOUNG LIFE OF PAT SUMMERALL

You are about to read about George Allen. No, not George Allen the Hall of Fame head coach famous for turning the Rams and Redskins into winners during the '60s and '70s. This is a Giants book after all. We're talking about George Allen "Pat" Summerall.

"Pat was a nickname," Summerall explained. "I was raised by an aunt and an uncle and they had a son named Mike. It was just like the Polish jokes that later became the subject of many joking stories. At that time it was the Irish [who were the butt of many jokes], and it was always Pat and Mike so we became Pat and Mike. Since his name was Mike they called me Pat."

Once Summerall reached the big city, the New York media tried to take credit for his nickname.

"When I got to New York and started to have success as a kicker, the New York media said Pat stood for 'Point After Touchdown,'" he laughed. "But that's obviously not true. I had that name for a long time."

Long before he reached the Giants, Summerall was a star on many levels. He captured the Florida state tennis championship at the age of 16. He also played football (as a two-way end), baseball, and ran track. Oh, and he was twice named All-State in basketball.

"I was the biggest kid in class so I was obligated to do everything," Summerall said.

And as for the kicking career that made him so famous, Summerall didn't kick for the first time until he was a sophomore at the University of Arkansas.

"Whoever they had kicking off wasn't doing a good job so they asked anyone who thought they could kick to come out (to practice) 15 minutes early," Summerall recalled. "So I went out early and I found out I could kick. I had not done any kicking before then."

Growing up, Summerall was greatly affected by two very special people during his youth.

"I lived with my grandmother (Augusta Georgia), who was a great influence on my life," he said. "She was a wonderful person. She taught me about values and what life was all about."

But she had help from one of Summerall's coaches as well.

"My high school coach (Jim Melton) had as much of an influence on my life as anybody," he said. "He turned me from a passive-type and shy person into being an aggressive participant in almost every sport. I give him a lot of credit. Without him I probably don't get to the level I did."

THE GAME OF MY LIFE
GIANTS VS. BROWNS—DECEMBER 14, 1958
BY PAT SUMMERALL

The most memorable game of my career was in 1958 at Yankee Stadium when I kicked a field goal to beat the Browns. That, of course, gave us the championship and sent us into the "Greatest Game Ever Played." But I don't know for sure if that was necessarily my best game. I had gotten hurt the week earlier against Detroit and there was some question whether I was even going to be able to kick or not. In fact, I didn't kick off that game because they were afraid that I'd get hurt. So that was definitely my most memorable, but it might not have been my greatest or best.

There were two games that next year—one against the (Chicago) Cardinals and one against the Steelers, when we won 9-3 and lost 14-9. Obviously the field goals I kicked were the only scoring in both games. I remember after those games Cliff Livingston asked me how it felt to be the Giants offense. Those were probably better games where I kicked off, did a better job of kicking, and played a little more.

Pat Summerall shows off his kicking shoe at Yankee Stadium on November 8, 1959, after kicking the New York Giants to a 9-3 win over the Chicago Cardinals. *AP Photos*

The game we won against the Cardinals, of course, stands out as a better memory. I *was* the only offense that day. That was when our defense really started to come into its own and the fans at Yankee Stadium started to recognize how good the defense was. That was Sam Huff,

(Andy) Robustelli, (Jim) Katcavage, (Dick) Modzelewski, Jimmy Patton, and all that bunch.

Also in 1959, there was a game when we beat the Rams in Los Angeles. I think it was the opening game of the season and we beat the Rams, 23-21, and I kicked three field goals. That might rank up with the rest of them because we won on the last play of the game.

The more successful you are, the more you think you're going to be successful. It's like putting in golf. Success breeds success. I think most fans and media have the idea that you're thinking about all the pressure and you're thinking about the situation before big kicks like the ones against the Rams and the Browns. But you're really not; you sort of block all that stuff out.

But as a kicker, you're always aware of the situation. Like against Los Angeles, you know that if you don't make it, you lose. You're aware of the magnitude of the situation. But you can't allow yourself to think about what's going to happen if you miss or if you make it. You don't think about those things. You just think about the pressure of the moment or the feeling of the moment. But you have that feeling of being by yourself, being totally alone. It's like you're in a capsule. You're not aware of the crowd or the situation. You just become aware of the things you have to do mechanically in that situation. You've done it so many times that it becomes a habit without it even being a habit. Things like, what you do with your ankle and what you do with your leg and remembering to do this and that. But you've done them all so many times they become like a habit and you don't really have to think about them. You just do them.

I know when I kicked that field goal against Cleveland in 1958 it was sort of a blur in my memory as to what I was feeling. I don't remember there being a big crowd, I don't really remember anything vivid about the situation. The weather that day was so bad. It had snowed and you couldn't even see the yard-line markers on the field. That was obviously a problem during the game and caused quite a problem kicking too.

We were at midfield and they sent me in to kick a very long field goal. All I remember is that when I walked into the huddle, Charlie Conerly, who was the quarterback and also the holder, looked up at me and asked, "What the heck are you doing here?" I said, "That's not really the way to build confidence, is it?"

Earlier in that game, I made one from about 46 yards. But that was going in the opposite direction, which was always more difficult to kick in at Yankee Stadium, going to left field. But I had missed from about 35 yards away on the series before the game-winner. I remember my teammates, particularly the guys on defense, telling me not to worry about it and that they would get me another chance. We had to win that game; a tie wouldn't help us. Having so many guys come over telling me that they'd get me another chance and not to worry about it was very memorable. I'll never forget the pats on the back and the reception when I got back to the sideline after making it. But most of it is all like a jumble these days.

I can see that kick—and probably all of them—going through the uprights to this day. Against the Browns, it was so far out that you had to hit it a certain way. If you hit it solid, it doesn't spin as often. It acts more like a knuckle ball coming from a pitcher because it's not spinning as much. The ball sort of breaks back and forth. I can still see it heading toward the left upright and then breaking back at the end towards the middle of the goalposts. I can still see Vinnie Swerc, who worked for the Giants for years, standing behind the goalpost with his arms out and catching it after it went through.

People believe that there is so much that goes through your mind that never actually does go through your mind when you're playing. You just sort of block everything out; it's kind of like being in a vacuum.

Once you start to be more successful, you become more confident. I remember earlier in my career at times when I was missing, I would hope the offense would make a first down so I didn't have to go in and kick a field goal. Then as I became successful, I remember hoping that they didn't make a first down so they would put it on me. At that point, you relish the pressure. You feel like you have a chance to produce and then when you do, it's a very great, exhilarating feeling.

When I made the field goal in Cleveland to win the championship, the first person I saw when I got off the field was (Vince) Lombardi, who grabbed me and hugged me. I thought he was going to say, "Great kick," or, "Wonderful job," or something like that. But all he said to me was, "You son of a bitch, you know you can't kick it that far." That was his way of congratulating me.

There's a funny story behind that ball, the one that actually went through for the win. I held onto it after the game and got all the guys to sign it. But years later when I was living in New Jersey, my kids needed a ball for the front-yard game so they took that ball. Of course it was wet outside at the time so all the names disappeared, but I still have the ball.

The memories from that game are vivid, but at the same time I don't really remember what it was like at the time. I remember going to the team party that night and being cheered as I walked into the room. I remember the happiness as I saw it go through; the feeling as I saw the kick was good. But there's really not that much else I recall about that kick.

That was a very special team to be on. That was the time and year that Sam Huff was discovered as the monster in the middle and that's when everyone started to realize how good the defense was. We won a lot of games with just defense. The offense had a tough time getting on track all year. They were just not a very effective offense, but the defense was great. We had Tom Landry coaching the defensive unit. He was my coach as well. I knew what a special man he was and what a great man he was. I didn't know he was going to turn out to be the legend that he became. But I sure knew he was brilliant. I was fortunate in that because I was playing both ways, I got to go to both meetings. The offensive meetings were run by Lombardi and the defense by Landry. So I got to learn from both of those guys in that one year. With those two, that was just about all you needed.

Being on the Giants meant so much to me. I would have never been in broadcasting if I hadn't played for the Giants. And if the Giants weren't good at that time, I probably never would have been auditioned by CBS, and I never would have gotten into broadcasting.

We were the toast of New York at that time. New York really discovered pro football and the Giants. I think that was the time when pro football started into the heyday that it still is in today. That's when television stations and viewers discovered that the game was made for T.V. That period is when pro football really started to become America's game.

It was great being in New York. We were the kings of New York. I don't remember ever buying a dinner or a drink anywhere during that whole time. It was like we were the Lords of Manhattan. It was a great feeling. But nobody was a bigger hero than anyone else. That's what made it really nice. Conerly was a hero, (Frank) Gifford was a hero, (Kyle) Rote was a hero, Sam Huff and Robustelli and all the defensive guys were recognizable and celebrities. We had the same group together almost every year. That was the great thing about it. I still keep in touch and talk with many of those guys today.

GAME RESULTS

After beginning the 1958 season with an 8-3 mark, the Giants needed to win their season finale against the Cleveland Browns in order to qualify for the playoffs. Even a tie in that contest wouldn't be good enough to extend Big Blue's season. As Pat Summerall explained, he was unable to break a 10-10 tie late in that contest when he misfired on a field-goal attempt. However, as his defense promised, they gave him another shot, and he connected on a 49-yarder. Summerall's kick turned out to be the game winner as the Giants defeated the Browns, 13-10, to reach the playoffs again two years after capturing their first NFL title.

The first playoff game the following week was a rematch with Cleveland. New York and its stellar defense shut down Jim Brown and the Browns by a 10-0 count. Cleveland's superstar back, who had rushed for a then-NFL record 1,527 yards that season, was held to only eight yards during the contest.

That led to New York and the Baltimore Colts squaring off in the 1958 NFL Championship game, also known as "The Greatest Game Ever Played." The Colts tied the game on a 20-yard Steve Myhra field goal with only seven seconds to play. Then, in the first sudden death overtime in an NFL championship game in league history, Baltimore took home the trophy when Alan Ameche plunged over from one yard out, giving the Colts a 23-17 victory.

Late Giants owner Wellington Mara had long credited Summerall's kick in the regular-season finale against the Browns as one of the most important plays in the history of the National Football League. According to Mara, without that kick, there is no New York presence in the playoffs and "The Greatest Game Ever Played," which totally transformed the league from a television, media, and fan standpoint, likely never unfolds.

Chapter 17

FRANK GIFFORD

THE YOUNG LIFE OF
FRANK GIFFORD

With no opponent having a chance to slow him down, only low grades kept Frank Gifford out of USC his freshman year. But with the help of legendary football coach Homer Beatty, Gifford went to Bakersfield College for a year, got back on track, and was an All-American for the Trojans in practically no time at all.

"Like so many kids, my high school coach had a major impact on me," said Gifford, who played for Beatty at Bakersfield High School. "Not only in football but I practically lived at his home. My mother and father were working in Alaska when I was in high school much of the time. He really became like a surrogate father."

Growing up, Gifford's father was an oil worker so he "lived all over the place." That's when Beatty stepped in and provided the structure Gifford was obviously missing.

"I could care less about going to school at the time and he got me involved academically," Gifford said of Beatty. "He had gone to USC and once he realized I could play at that level he talked me into getting more involved academically than I had ever been. From there it was on to USC."

After a Hall of Fame football career where he became one of the most recognizable and popular players in the storied history of the New York Football Giants, Gifford said he owes it all to Beatty.

"I've never forgotten all he's done for me," he said. "Sometimes when I think back I wonder if I didn't have him what could have happened in my life. Maybe I'd own an oil field or something like that. I could have followed my father's footsteps or my brother's. They did very well. But I wouldn't have known the New York I know and gotten to win the championship that I did. Life certainly would have been different without him."

THE GAME OF MY LIFE
GIANTS VS. BEARS—NFL CHAMPIONSHIP,
DECEMBER 30, 1956
BY FRANK GIFFORD

It wasn't too long ago and I was on the phone with Sam Huff and we were laughing about a couple of the Redskins games in the '50s. We had a couple of those games where we just beat the hell out of them. Everything worked. It was a couple of nearly perfect games where we beat them pretty badly. We were all in some type of zone and that was around when we ended up going on to win the championship in 1956. These were games I recall when everything just came together for us. I think I might have even thrown a touchdown in one or two of those games. I actually threw a lot of them through the years.

We didn't like those guys much and they didn't like us either. The Redskins had always been a long-time rival of the Giants before I even got here, which was a long time ago. I remember the Redskins owner at the time (George Preston Marshall) and the Maras not getting along so well either. It was the two major cities and two of the bigger franchises at that time.

In those games I know I threw, ran, and caught touchdowns, maybe even all in one game. Again, everything we did worked for us. But that whole season in '56 everything seemed to be clicking for us. That was the third year of Lombardi and it all came together. We had the right people and the right offense. We won the championship, 47-7. That might still be one of the biggest spreads in NFL championship history.

That game was another great memory for me. What stands out about that one is that it might have been a different game if we didn't

---

During his time in New York, Frank Gifford was a seven-time Pro Bowler at three different positions. *AP Images*

score on the first drive. It was a really cold and bitter day. It was only like nine degrees out. They had a real good defensive team and we were facing something like a third-and-12. I beat my guy on an out pattern. Don Heinrich hit me and the defender slipped on the ice. We picked up the first down and we took that first drive in for a touchdown. They were really out of the game after that first drive. I remember that I scored the last touchdown of that game.

I played in five championship games and that was the only one we won. We won in '56, but then we lost in '58, we lost in '59, we lost in '61, which I didn't play in, and then we lost again in '62 and '63. It meant so much because the Giants hadn't won in so long. I think the previous championship was in the '30s (1938).

That team was especially memorable because it really was the first time anyone had coached defense like Tom Landry. With him as your defensive coordinator and Vince Lombardi as your offensive coordinator, and a head coach (Jim Lee Howell) that stayed out of the way, it was a dream situation, especially when you're a key part of the offense.

We were a much more closely-knit group than the Giants and NFL teams are today. No one made a whole heck of a lot of money. Most of us came from somewhere else and were now living in New York. A lot of us lived in the same hotel. Our wives knew each other, our kids knew each other. Today, guys are scattered all over the place. We got to know each other not only as players, but as family guys and friends. Some of those friendships still remain. I'm still really close with Sam Huff, Harland Svare, and Cliff Livingston, especially.

It was a lot more fun than it would be today. These guys make a heck of a lot more money than we did and all that, but I think we enjoyed it a lot more than they ever could. It was just a different world.

Everyone always talks about me playing offense, but when Lombardi came to the Giants in 1954 I had been playing defense as well. The year before that I had played both ways and they really didn't quite know what to do with me. I had played both ways at USC, too, and was named All-Conference as both a defensive back and a running back. When I got to the Giants they still weren't sure what was going to happen to (former No. 1 draft pick) Kyle Rote, who had been hurt. They decided to draft me, and the plan was if Kyle played, I could play defense and if he didn't I'd play offense. Kyle limped through a couple years so I ended up playing both ways. But when Lombardi got there, the first words he ever said to me were, "You're my halfback." That was the end of my defensive career; I never played that again. It really wasn't that disappointing having to stop playing defense. Not at all.

But I actually enjoyed playing defense because Tom Landry was our defensive coach at that time. I learned an enormous amount of football playing defense under Tom Landry. He was the first one to really put some scientific effort into building a defense. In turn, knowing how to play defense so well helped me out on offense.

When Tom Landry went to Dallas and became the head coach, I was still playing. I came back and played wide receiver my final three years. We used to reverse all his keys against him all the time. We just beat the hell out of them one of his first years down in Dallas. For instance, if I were the flanker to the right and the back on that side ran a circle, that would mean the outside back generally would make an out move. We just reversed it on him. We'd circle (Alex) Webster and I'd make an end move. Landry had his defensive backs so well-trained to read those keys that the guy on me was expecting an out move so when I went inside it was a piece of cake. We just reversed Tom's keys on him and beat him 41-10. To beat a Landry-coached team by that much you had to be doing something right.

Lombardi built that offense around me and then he later went to Green Bay and built the same offense around Paul Hornung. In that offense the left halfback was the primary weapon. I threw the ball, caught the ball, ran the ball. It was a lot of fun playing for him. I used to kid Paul all the time that he was me, but just bigger. I used to cover him on television and he became a really good friend of mine and he still is.

Being a Giant meant everything in the world to me. I stayed in New York all year round. I missed the 1961 season, but at that time I was already doing my own radio show and was doing the news on local television. When I came back in 1962 to play my final three seasons, I continued to do my TV show while I was playing. I went right out of one and into the other. I talked to Tiki (Barber) about it several years ago and it seems like he did almost exactly what I did. He played 10 years and I played nine before I came back. I just missed it after being out in '61 and came back. I knew I could do everything that I was already doing in television. If he follows suit, after his year off he's going to come back and play three years as a wide receiver. Ha! He's followed everything else I've done, but I don't think he'll be doing that.

The game is so much different today. They used Tiki a lot differently than I was used. He was the primary running back. There were several seasons that I led the team in both running and receiving. That's just a different world. I've kidded him many times about him breaking my Giants records. In anything, records don't last forever. I was very proud mine lasted as long as they did. I think I still have one standing, for most touchdowns. It's pretty amazing that it has lasted for so long.

While it was black and white and two different worlds between playing the game and announcing for it, I had an easy transition because I started while I was still playing. I originally started on the announcing side filling in for Phil Rizzuto. His producer asked me to try some of it for myself. I had done some local television out in California and had studied acting. I had been under contract with Warner Brothers, so it wasn't like it was a different world for me. When they asked me to fill in for Phil Rizzuto, it was a piece of cake, and then I realized how financially rewarding it was for me as well. So I started to focus on the television side of it and did my own pregame show first. Then I did some local news. From there, I graduated to full-time local news and reporting and then covering games. Then when *Monday Night Football* rolled around, Roone Arledge brought me over from CBS and as they say, that's it. I did 27 years of *Monday Night Football* and probably more prime-time T.V. than anyone in the history of television. I got to stay in the game that I loved and at a level that was pretty extraordinary in its own right. No one thought football on television was going to work and it more than worked because we ruled the airwaves for a while. The game's been good to me.

GAME RESULTS

As Gifford alluded to, the Giants pounded the Redskins pretty good a bunch of times in the '50s. First there was New York's 51-21 victory in D.C. in 1954. The next year Big Blue blasted Washington in New York by a 35-7 count. The teams split their season series in mostly close games during the 1956 and 1957 seasons before the Giants blew the Redskins' doors off a couple more times in New York—1958 by a 30-0 score and a 45-14 victory the following year.

In the 1956 NFL Championship Game, the Giants smashed Chicago, 47-7. It was the Giants' first championship in 18 years and it was a cakewalk. Fullback Mel Triplett capped New York's opening drive with a 17-yard touchdown run. A pair of Ben Agajanian field goals extended the lead to 13-0 and the Giants had a stranglehold on the game by halftime when they led 34-7. Two short touchdown runs by Alex Webster and Henry Moore's recovery of a blocked punt in the end zone established New York's halftime cushion. In the second half, Charlie Conerly connected on two touchdown passes—a nine-yarder to Kyle Rote and a 14-yarder to Frank Gifford—that forged the final score.

Chapter 18

GEORGE MARTIN

THE YOUNG LIFE OF GEORGE MARTIN

George Martin certainly didn't have high aspirations as he left to begin what turned out to be a record-breaking 14-year career with the Giants. Heck, he didn't even think he was going to make it out of training camp his rookie season.

"I was very humble," Martin said. "I had no inclination that I could play pro ball at all."

You could even ask his wife, Dianne.

"This is what I said to my wife when I left for training camp," Martin continued. "I went to school to be a teacher, I majored in education, and I said, 'Honey, I'm going to training camp and I'll see you in a couple weeks, maybe less. But maybe I could stick it out a couple weeks. Then I'll be back and I'll finish up school and then we'll get on with the rest of our lives and I'll become a schoolteacher.'"

Not so fast. Martin couldn't have been more misguided about his future.

"And 14 years later . . . " he laughed.

Growing up, all Martin was looking to do was become an art teacher on either the grade school or high school level. His only other desire? To be just like dear old dad.

"I wanted my dad's character," he said. "That's what I always tried to emulate. Even though he didn't know anything about football, he was a share-cropper and he worked for the United States military. But my dad always had outstanding character and people always spoke fondly and very warmly about him. I always wanted to have those kinds of warm adulations hurled in my direction as well. I always admired my dad."

But he credits his mom, Janie, for his aggressiveness and athletic traits.

"I always said that I got my athletic demeanor from my mom because she was the disciplinarian in the family," he said.

And George wasn't the only athlete Janie Martin produced. George's younger brother, Doug, played 10 seasons as a defensive end for the Minnesota Vikings.

"She raised two sons that played a combined 24 years in the NFL so that's not too bad," George Martin said.

THE GAME OF MY LIFE
GIANTS VS. BRONCOS—NOVEMBER 23, 1986
BY GEORGE MARTIN

I'm not quite sure how to categorize what my best game would have been. I don't think I have that kind of objectivity, but there are a few games that I'm extremely proud of. There was one game where we played the New Orleans Saints down in New Orleans and I recorded four sacks in that game. To me that was unprecedented; I had never done that before. That stands out as a milestone individual accomplishment during the course of a game.

There were at least a couple of occasions where I had three quarterback sacks. That's always the mark of accomplishment for a defensive end. There was another three-sack game in Seattle. There was one game against the Washington Redskins where I caused the game-winning fumble that Troy Archer picked up and returned back, which I was very proud of. And also actually scoring seven touchdowns throughout my career was great. All of those are to me spectacular moments.

It's tough to look at one game and say it was your best, because there are a lot of things we look at as players. I may have had a great day rushing

---

After getting drafted in the 11th round, George Martin didn't think he'd play 14 seasons for New York. *Andy Hayt, Getty Images*

the quarterback but then played the run like crap. Then it would be tough to say that was a great game.

But I'd have to say the game against the Denver Broncos when I went 78 yards and scored a touchdown was a big occurrence and a big event for me, only because of the importance of it and the time when it took place, which was during our Super Bowl year. That would probably be my biggest moment. That one's a lot easier to identify and quantify for me. It was so memorable because the interception was against (John) Elway and because it was such an improbability that it was returned 78 yards if you consider who was carrying the ball.

Of course getting the safety in the Super Bowl is something that will always stand out as a stand-alone accomplishment because it took place under some pretty marvelous conditions and a pretty fantastic occasion. That obviously led to our victory and that will also be something that you can always say was a good moment in time.

But the Denver touchdown was the biggest touchdown of my career, without question. That play was pivotal in our run to the Super Bowl. That to me was the most memorable single event in my whole career.

The improbability of going 78 yards—all the stars would have had to align for something like that to occur. As fortune would have it, they did. We got some great blocks, guys were hustling and despite Lawrence's lunacy during that run everyone contributed to the success of that play. If you remember that play, Lawrence (Taylor) was asking for the ball. My first inclination, of course, was to give it to someone who was faster than I was. That included my entire defensive team and even a few of the referees. But I thought better of it because when I was going to lateral the ball, John Elway was actually between Lawrence and me. I could just see (Bill) Parcells having a meltdown if I had a turnover and gave the ball back. I thought better of it, so I took it in myself.

I was kind of skeptical the entire run that I was going to be able to score. I thought John Elway was a better tackler than that, but that's what you get for assuming. He had a pretty good angle on me, but I guess he wasn't in a defensive mood that day. Then I figured it would only be a matter of time until a wide receiver caught up with me and tripped me up. But that never happened. I just kept chugging down and I remember at the last moment, Mark Collins came down and one of Denver's offensive linemen had caught up with me and he had put himself between me and the goal line. Mark made a great block that some may call a clip. But that was the last big contribution that got me into the end zone.

I remember once I crossed the goal line the lights went out for me. Lawrence jumped on me and kind of horse-collared me and then the rest of my teammates came and jumped on me and actually blocked out the sun. I was down there already gasping for air and all I kept saying was, "Get off me, get off me, I can't breathe." I had just ran 78 yards, I was emotionally drained, I was physically tired, and I had half of my teammates piled on top of me. That was the greatest event of my career. I'm certain of it.

The capper of it all is that of all the games that my dad had ever seen, of which there weren't too many in Giants Stadium, he was at that game. So I gave him that ball that night. That was a father-son moment for the ages. That made it mean even more for me. It was special to me because my dad was a quiet supporter of mine. The specter of pro football was kind of awe-inspiring to him. He was kind of like a kid when they first go to Disneyland. You always say you want to do something special for your parents or your dad to make it special for him. But I couldn't have possibly thought that's what I would end up doing for him.

That was the proudest I've ever seen my father of me. Dad wasn't too emotional, but he was very proud of me that day. When he saw that the entire stadium of 76,000 people was standing up cheering and that it was his son down there causing the commotion, he was speechless. That rarely happens to my dad. Then when I gave him the football, you couldn't have offered him a billion dollars for that ball.

Bill Parcells was so superstitious that he started inviting my dad to all the games and bringing him along to the games because he wanted my dad to be there. My dad didn't mind that at all.

The ironic thing is that after the game, Bill said that that was the greatest play he had ever seen, especially for a defensive lineman. That was his quote. He said that I was terrific and that he hoped I'd play for another five years. I remember all that because they caught it all on film. But the ironic thing is that when I got to the end zone and I have all this humanity on me and I can't move, Bill's yelling at me to get off the field. Here I just made the greatest play of my career and all he's yelling about is to get off the field so we didn't get a penalty. I thought that was ironic, but that was typical Bill. He put things in perspective real quick.

It's funny because I really don't remember much about that game other than that play. That one play basically encapsulated that entire game. I do remember Brad Benson saying just before that play to "keep your eye on Martin" because I was lined up near our sideline. He said I was going to do something special. I still don't know where he got that premonition from. He was talking to a couple guys on the sideline. He came up to me after the game and said that he warned everyone to keep their eyes on me. I had no idea what was going on. He told me after the game and I said, "Boy, Brad, you should say that more often."

That play, in and of itself, was the entire game. It was a moment in time that'll always stand out. To me, the game started when I intercepted the ball and when I got into the end zone, the game stopped. It was just so special. I never came down off that cloud. I never did.

Besides that play I really don't remember anything else. I have a really bad memory. My wife calls it a selective memory. When you have 14 years of NFL experience, it leaves you a lot of stuff to forget. It amazes me when I listen to these baseball players and they're talking about past games and they knew what inning it was and what kind of pitch it was. Those guys are out of their mind. I never had that ability to recall. I marvel at the people who can, but I'm not one of them.

I do remember people talking about how slow I ran. I said that when I caught the ball I remember the sun was shining and it was a nice, bright, sunny day. By the time I had gotten to the end zone, it had turned dark and clouded over. That's how long it took me to get to the end zone.

That game really set the stage for the showdown in the Super Bowl. I think up until that point there was some uncertainty as to how good we really were because the Broncos, at that point, were a very formidable team. We had some questions whether we could stop John Elway, who was the talk of the whole NFL at that time. We withstood the litmus test, which gave us confidence going into the Super Bowl against Denver.

Winning that Super Bowl was fantastic. I have tried since that day to summarize what it has meant to me and I haven't been successful at doing it yet. I had been in the league 12 years at that point. You have no idea all the bad stuff that happened to the Giants: we lost eight consecutive games one year, people were burning their tickets, the fact that we had the fumble at the Meadowlands, we were involved in the worst performance in the history of *Monday Night Football.*

There was so much negativity and so much bad history that I had been a part of with the Giants. I saw so many of my teammates give up on the Giants and say, "Hey, I want to go to a winner," and, "I should be traded," and all that stuff. And I was always optimistic. I thought that I probably could go somewhere else and at least win a division or something like that. But I thought how sweet it would be if we could do it right here after all those years.

I remember when we were introduced before the game at Pasadena. When you saw the sea of red, white, and blue, when you saw all those fans, when you saw your parents, your family, and all of your supporters that had stood by you undyingly all those years it meant so much. And when the game was over I had never seen so many macho men—so many fathers, uncles, and brothers crying in the stands—I can't even describe it. It was a defining moment in so many people's lives. Other than seeing my son born, I can't tell you anything that even comes close to it.

GAME RESULTS

No one knew it at the time but this contest was a preview of Super Bowl XXI. That was good news for the Giants and their fans as Big Blue was being outplayed early on in this one. But that's when big number 75 took over. With the Broncos leading 6-3 and nearing New York's red zone, Martin picked off John Elway's flare pass and returned it 78 yards down the sideline. That single play turned the momentum of the game—and possibly the entire season—in New York's favor.

And the always hard-to-impress Bill Parcells was even, well, impressed.

"That was the greatest football play I've ever seen," Parcells told multiple New York newspapers following the game.

Even though the Broncos knotted up the score at 16 on a Sammy Winder touchdown run in the fourth quarter, the Giants were not to be denied. On their final, game-winning drive, Phil Simms converted a third-and-21 with a 24-yard pass to Bobby Johnson and then connected with Phil McConkey for a 46-yard gain. That set up Raul Allegre to drill a 34-yard field goal with only six seconds to play for a 19-16 victory.

Joe Morris led the ground attack with 106 rushing yards, but this game was won via the not-so-fleet feet of George Martin. The victory was New York's fifth in a row amid a streak that reached 12 and ended with the 39-20 win over those same Broncos in Super Bowl XXI two months later.

Chapter 19

ROMAN OBEN

THE YOUNG LIFE OF ROMAN OBEN

Talk about being a fan of your hometown team. Roman Oben practically grew up on the Washington Redskins, so much that he sold hot pretzels at Redskins games for three years while he was in high school.

Born in Cameroon, West Africa, he moved with his mother, Marie, to D.C. when he was four years old. Oben's mother came to the United States to work for the Cameroon Embassy.

However, she wasn't a big fan of her son strapping on the helmet and shoulder pads, so Roman didn't begin playing organized football until he was 15 years old. By that time, he had already logged three seasons working concessions at RFK Stadium.

"I made 50 bucks a game," he said. "I could have made more but I'd always cash out at the end of the third quarter so I could watch the end of the game. I always enjoyed watching football. I'd always get changed and hang out where the players would come out and everyone always used to think I was some player's kid or something. I always thought that was funny."

To this day, Oben never forgets how he was first introduced to the NFL—and he hopes to see another youngster soon enjoy a similarly fortunate fate.

"Every game, especially when we're playing against the Redskins, I see kids walking up and down those stairs selling stuff," he said. "I wonder who could be the next kid to be the next pro football player. My story—someone in the next 25 years is going to have that same story as I did."

THE GAME OF MY LIFE
GIANTS AT BUCCANEERS—SEPTEMBER 12, 1999
BY ROMAN OBEN

That Tampa game on opening day in 1999 was a really big game for me. It was my fourth year, it was my free agent year, and I really needed to solidify myself with a strong performance against that defense. You always hear about a three-headed monster on offense. Well, they had a three-headed monster defensively with Warren Sapp, (Derrick) Brooks, and John Lynch.

That was the only game of my Giants career that I got MVP of the game offensively, as opposed to the whole offense or the offensive line as a group getting it, and just me receiving one of those balls. The coaches named me offensive MVP because of how well I graded out that game. We only had 107 yards of offense in that game but we still won. That was the game that (Trent) Dilfer ran out of bounds and threw one up for grabs that Percy Ellsworth picked off.

When you consider that it was my fourth year in the league and third as a starter, that game and that season was a very big deal to me. (Former Giants GM) George Young had drafted me to replace Jumbo Elliott. While the fans didn't understand it at the time because I was a barely 300-pound guy from Louisville, it all made sense. George Young knew that you had to build through the draft and just complement your team with older free-agent signings. That's what A.J. Smith did in San Diego. The quick fix of signing a bunch of free agents so rarely works.

We had played Tampa the previous two years and had lost both times. In 1997 they beat us at home (20-8) and in '98 they beat us at their place (20-3). It was starting to become a little bit of an NFC rivalry. We won the division in '97, then went 8-8 the next year. So, 1999 was the year we were supposed to turn it around and put it all together. After playing against that defense, if you did well, you knew you were going to be good. At least you knew you were decent enough that you should be

---

Offensive lineman Roman Oben (72) was a native of Cameroon, West Africa, before making the move to America as a child.
Tom Hauck, Getty images

a good football team. Sapp was having huge seasons and the rest of that defense was pretty tough.

I remember recognizing the importance of that game long before it came and preparing more than usual for it. I watched so much tape because I really didn't know who I would be going up against. You knew first-round pick Regan Upshaw was eventually going to start, but in the meantime you had Steve White and this guy Marcus Jones at the other end. It really wasn't about Warren Sapp as much as it was that you're going against a guy that you don't really read or hear about and you know that he's going to bring his lunch pail to work and give you a good, solid 15 rounds. I prepared for Steve White just as if he were Reggie White.

I just felt different that game. I really felt like I had already played that game before. Every blitz that game, I knew it was coming. Everything the defense tried to throw at me, I was ready for. It was like I played the game during the week from watching film. I just felt like anything short of a tornado or lightning striking in the middle of the field I would have been prepared for. That's a great feeling when you're out on the field.

We won the game and I played very consistently. You could say that they gave the game MVP to an offensive lineman because the offense wasn't that good. Or you could say we couldn't move the ball because their defense was so good and to even get some consistency from an offensive lineman was impressive. I believe the latter was the reason I got MVP.

I was on such a high after that game. I got injured and tore my meniscus during that game, but I was able to play through it the rest of the season. It was an incredible high; I was still only 26 years old. I felt like I had really arrived in the NFL after that game.

During my first year starting in 1997 no one really knew about me, so playing well was kind of looked at as a bit of a pleasant surprise. The next year I just built on the previous season. By 1999, everyone in the division and the conference knew about me. Lions head coach Rod Marinelli, who was the Bucs defensive line coach back then, told me that they voted for me for the Pro Bowl that year. The Tampa team had me as one of the top three tackles that year. All of that came from that game on opening day. That game really carried me about five weeks that season. No matter how bad a game I might have had around midseason, everyone still remembered how I played in the season opener against Tampa. That game really started my whole career. But the shame was that we weren't winning consistently that season.

After that game our fullback Charles Way said some nice things to me. He was telling me that we had a good offensive line and that I needed to be the leader of it. I kind of felt like I was getting knighted to become the leader of the O-line. I had always looked up to Ron Stone because he came from Dallas as a free agent and he had a few years on me. I think that was the game that—not that I didn't look up to Stone anymore—I felt like guys were now looking up to me for leadership.

You feel better about yourself after that type of game because you know that you're part of the solution and not the problem. It's great to have a game like that where you're blocking well, you're running guys to the sideline, and you're running downfield trying to nail some defensive back at the end of the play. As a result, you start to carry yourself differently because not only are you now a part of the solution but you're even doing a little more than your job, a little more than expected. You get to the point where you're in a nice little comfort zone, a nice flow.

There were a couple other games that stand out, both coming during my second season in 1997.

First off was the Redskins game at home when we clinched the NFC East. The first time we played them during the season Ken Harvey had four sacks against us. Even though I only really gave up one of them, when the guy lined up on you gets that many, it sure doesn't look too good for you. But in that second game at home, with us going for the division, there was no way that I was going to be singled out for any sacks. We ran the ball well and took care of them. It was very emotional for me; I was still a young guy. Plus you knew everyone was watching that game. That was one of those games where I knew everyone from back home in the D.C. area was going to be watching and surely my high school coach as well. So you really wanted to do well.

It was a great feeling to clinch the division and have that feeling that you're going to the playoffs. And at my position I felt like a really big piece of the puzzle. When you talk about football positions you're talking about left tackle, cornerback, and quarterback. Those are the key spots on a team. Playing without those guys would be like having a map of America without Texas, California, and Florida.

Then we played the Vikings in the Wild Card game and looked to be moving on to play Green Bay the next week but we collapsed and lost that game. Ron Jaworski told me that if we would have held on and won the Minnesota playoff game in 1997, considering how well I played against John Randle on a national stage in my first year of starting, that could have done exactly for me what Tony Boselli going against Bruce Smith did for Boselli early in his career. It would have shown me performing at a high level in a key situation against a superstar. But we lost the lead and the game and that was the end of that. I'm not saying I was going to make a bunch of Pro Bowls off that one game, but it might have gone a long way toward me becoming more of a household name in the league.

That was my first year starting, and we were the first team to go undefeated in the NFC East that season. With me going against Randle, who moved from tackle to end that year, it was the game's marquee matchup. I had confidence that I could shut him down no matter what he did. He was talking crap to me before the game and trying to intimidate me. He found me before the national anthem and stood right in front of me. He was staring at me and doing all that nonsense like jumping up and down. He was acting like he was in a high school movie about football. He was that kind of guy. But I played him well and kept him quiet during the game.

We were on our way that game. We were up 19-3 at the half and 22-13 late in the game and were just waiting to play Green Bay, which is where we would have gone the next week. But then it all fell apart on us. It's unfortunate we didn't move on because we played well enough to win for most of the game.

GAME RESULTS

As the Giants offense struggled trying to get on track against the ferocious Bucs defense, that unit got some much-needed help from its counterparts. The Big Blue defense scored twice en route to a 17-13 opening-day victory in Tampa Bay.

On the Bucs' opening possession, Jessie Armstead sacked Trent Dilfer and forced a fumble that defensive tackle Christian Peter recovered and returned 38 yards for a touchdown. However, Tampa put up a field goal and a TD in the second quarter to take a 10-7 lead into halftime.

In the third quarter, Brad Maynard's 52-yard punt pinned the Bucs at their own one-yard line. On third down, rookie cornerback Andre

Weathers picked off a Dilfer pass and returned it eight yards for the go-ahead touchdown. New York's defense held on via three fourth-quarter interceptions—two by safety Percy Ellsworth and one from cornerback Phillippi Sparks, which sealed the game with only 1:24 to play.

The Giants won despite amassing only 107 total yards, one third-down conversion (out of 14 opportunities), and four total first downs.

In the victory over Washington during the '97 season, the Giants rolled to their first NFC East championship since 1990 with a 30-10 demolition of the Redskins. Charles Way's 15-yard touchdown run and Jason Sehorn's 35-yard interception return for a score were among the highlights.

Then, in the fateful Wild Card loss to the Vikings, Oben basically shut down perennial Pro Bowler John Randle, but the Giants allowed a nine-point lead to evaporate in the final two minutes and dropped a 23-22 stunner.

Chapter 20

TUCKER FREDERICKSON

THE YOUNG LIFE OF TUCKER FREDERICKSON

If Tucker Frederickson's life unfolded as he expected, he would have followed in his father's footsteps and would have become a veterinarian. However, he benefited from growing up in Florida where he could "play sports all the time," and before he knew it, he was a number one overall draft pick and heading to the Big Apple to play football.

"I went to Auburn to be a veterinarian, but then I got a chance to go to New York and that was it," Frederickson recalled.

Frederickson said that thanks to his father, Dr. Ivan, he had it pretty good as a child.

"My upbringing was not difficult; it was easy," he said. "We weren't rich but we weren't poor."

While he'll always be known at Auburn for playing both ways with equal aplomb on the gridiron, Frederickson was pretty accomplished at the shot put as well.

"I played everything in high school and then in college I threw the shot put actually. But that was just to get out of spring practice," he laughed. "I came in third or fourth in the SEC. I could throw it, but I knew I wasn't going to the Olympics. I liked throwing the shot put."

He also liked playing football, which he wasn't certain he could handle at the professional level until he actually proved it to himself.

"I didn't really know for sure that I belonged until the first practice and first exhibition game," he said. "You get in there and then you know you could play. I've never really been a real confident guy. I just had to prove it to myself as well as to other people. You have to go find out. You know rather quickly but even then you sort of have to move into it slowly."

THE GAME OF MY LIFE
GIANTS VS. EAGLES—OCTOBER 17, 1965
BY TUCKER FREDERICKSON

I would have to say that playing my first game in Yankee Stadium in New York had to be the highlight of my career. It was so exciting and so thrilling and so rewarding. There were a couple good games that I had in the stadium that I'll always remember. In 1970, I had a big game against the Redskins, but that was more of a statistically good game.

But the 1965 season was really what I'll always remember. It was my rookie year and the quarterback was Earl Morrall, who we acquired late in the preseason from Detroit. Everyone and everything sort of came together that year and we had a 7-7 season, but we were actually a lot better than that.

I had a couple good games that season against the Pittsburgh Steelers and the Chicago Cardinals. I had a great season as a rookie. I wound up in the Pro Bowl. The great Jim Brown was the other fullback in the Pro Bowl for us that year so I was pretty honored and thrilled to be able to be included with him. In my way of thinking, he was the best football player who ever lived. That entire season was a great season for me.

I know my buddy Sam Huff said he enjoyed playing against Jim Brown through the years. But that's actually how Sam became famous. Sure, Jim would run him over all the time, but he still got famous for being run over. Of course I'm joking about that. Sam's a good guy and he was a great player as well.

Playing against the Eagles in Yankee Stadium was the first game I ever played in the stadium. I had a couple good runs and we beat them so that was a very important game to me. Having a good game and winning in my first home game will always mean the world to me.

I remember later that season breaking loose against the Cardinals. For me, 50 yards is a long run and I think I had one of those in that game.

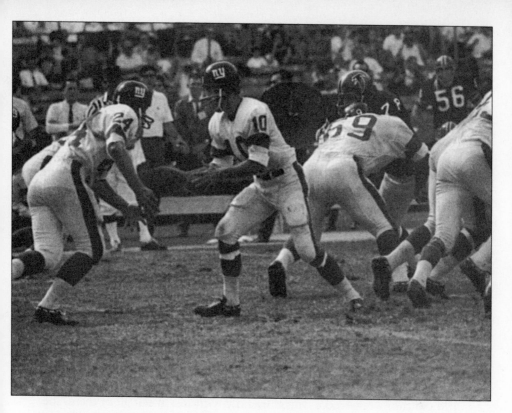

Running back Tucker Frederickson (24) had a successful career in New York despite only playing for one winning team.
Diamond Images, Getty Images

I scored on a run in which (Hall of Fame safety) Larry Wilson came up to tackle me. I lowered my shoulder on him and he bounced back pretty good.

But playing that first one in Yankee Stadium was huge. It didn't really sink in until after you were at the stadium, and it was already the middle of the game before you realized that you were actually playing at Yankee Stadium. You're looking around and seeing the monuments in centerfield. And the crowd back then was a very sophisticated crowd. People got real dressed up. It was a real upscale crowd. The memories of the stadium are huge. I was certainly in awe of it. And it was even more impressive once you got in there.

It was an unbelievable experience being introduced there as well. The announcer (Bob Sheppard) was great. His voice was incredible. Coming out of the dugout and being introduced was unbelievable. And to look up into the crowd and see how well everyone was dressed was really nice, too. Today, most people come to the games in jeans and T-shirts. It certainly was a different era and a different game than it is today. It was a great time to be in New York and a great time to be a part of a great organization, which the Giants certainly are.

Being introduced was always a thrill. Coming out of the dugout, they always lined you up before you ran out. Back then the goalposts were on the goal line so you always had to go under or around them when you were running out. Then to come out to such a wonderful ovation after being announced as a starter was unbelievable.

I was pretty confident in myself by that early point in the season. I realized very early on and by the end of the exhibition games I knew that I could play at this level. It certainly helped to have a good game, but from the first scrimmage and exhibition game in camp, you realize that you can play in the league. I wasn't quite as concerned about being able to play as I was in awe of the stadium and the history of the stadium.

I was pretty much accepted by my teammates right away. The veterans check you out early and if they know you can play, you become one of the boys. That basically happens your first time out there on the field. Within a few weeks, you're friendly with just about all of them. Joe Morrison turned out to be a really good friend early on, and a lot of them became friends to me later on. If you can play, they'll know it. That was something that I was concerned about but it happened fairly quickly. They want you to be good and want you to help so they're not going to give you too much of a hard time. If you can't play they're going to know it quickly.

We were 7-7 my first season after being 2-10-2 the year before. We played the Cowboys the last game and we got beat (38-20) or we would have been in second place. Had we won, we would have finished 8-6 and been in the playoffs. We would have been in the runner-up bowl in Miami. There was a runner-up bowl in addition to the championship game back then. But Dallas beat us and we ended up 7-7 and just missed it. But it was still just a great year all around.

We always all got together after the games, which was usually a lot of fun. It was a great group of guys. My house became the place to go after games so everybody used to show up there. We went back there and always got together. I had a place in Manhattan on 65th and 1st, and that was our beginning stop before we hit the town on Sunday nights.

We used to go to P.J. Clarke's and all the other famous joints like Toots Shor's, but it was basically Clarke's on Sunday nights. It was a great time to be a Giant and a wonderful time to be in New York. It was fantastic.

Playing in the city and the kind of reception you got from the city and the people you met were just incredible. Part of playing football back then was about meeting people. Today they don't have to worry about that as much because they all make so much money. But back then it was important. I stayed in the city in the off-season to work. We had to work in addition to playing back then.

GAME RESULTS

The Giants began the 1965 season with four consecutive road games. Big Blue came home for its home opener with a 2-2 mark. Tucker Frederickson's stats were modest during his first home contest, but he was likely just still in awe of playing in Yankee Stadium. Frederickson had a long gain of 11 yards among his 10 carries as the Giants broke out to a 35-7 lead and then had to hold on to defeat the Eagles, 35-27.

Frederickson fared much better statistically in the other two games he recalled from his Pro Bowl rookie season. On Halloween against the Cardinals, he had a long run of 41 yards among his 95 total yards for the game. He also rushed for a touchdown and caught an 11-yard pass as New York knocked off St. Louis by a 14-10 count. That victory gave the Giants a 4-3 record at the time.

Perhaps Frederickson's best game of his rookie campaign came against the Steelers on December 5, 1965. Frederickson was instrumental in New York's 35-10 rout of Pittsburgh that afternoon. He scored three times in that contest, twice on runs and once on a catch. He tallied 97 yards on 20 total touches with a long run of 15 yards and a long reception of 19 yards. Big Blue's victory over the Steelers improved the Giants' mark to 6-6 as they would finish the season .500 in between seasons in which they combined to win only three games (two in 1964 and one in 1966).

Chapter 21

BRIAN KELLEY

THE YOUNG LIFE OF BRIAN KELLEY

Thank heavens for Mama Lil. After all, where would the three Kelley boys have ended up without her? It's quite certain to say that Brian, the middle child, would most likely not be able to discuss his 11-year Giants career, that's for sure.

Mama Lil was the affectionate name given to Kelley's grandmother, who was called upon to raise all three Kelley boys.

"My parents left me when I was two years old," Kelley said. "I knew my dad, but I only saw him every so often, and my mom would come visit every once in a while. My grandmother raised me growing up in Dallas. Actually I lived in Lancaster, which was about 20 miles south of Dallas."

It was there that Mama Lil did her best to make men out of the Kelley boys.

"She meant everything to me," Kelley said. "I lived basically 14 years of my life with her. She was the only one ever there. We lived on welfare till I was 15. She had no money; she was poor. Me and my two brothers, one younger and one older, we didn't know what to do. We tried to help when we could, but we were all too young to help. And she was too old to do a lot."

But she did the best she could, which meant the world to Kelley.

"She was really the only strong point in my life and she kept us all focused," he said. "Without her, we could have gone anywhere. But she

151

put us straight real quick. She'd get out a switch and beat our asses if need be. She kept us going to school when that kind of situation easily could have gone in a different direction."

Kelley's father attempted to re-enter the picture once his son had made it big. Kelley was surprised, to say the least, when he saw his father after several years.

"I had not seen my dad since I was 14," he recalled. "Before my first game with the Giants back in Dallas, the *Dallas Morning News* had a big article about the local boy's homecoming and how the home boy made it good. Somehow my dad had read the paper and found out about it."

Never in his wildest dreams did Kelley envision his father would come calling.

"I was at the Marriott where the team was staying and rooming with Jack Gregory and there was a knock at my room door," he said. "So I get up and open the door and I'm just looking at this guy. He said, 'Brian, I'm your father. Don't you remember me? I'm your dad.' I had no idea who he was. I hadn't seen him in seven years."

But mostly thanks to Mama Lil, Brian Kelley would spend the next 11 years manning the middle of the Giants defense.

THE GAME OF MY LIFE
GIANTS AT REDSKINS—DECEMBER 19, 1982
BY BRIAN KELLEY

I would say the Redskins game back in 1982 was my best game. It came during the strike-shortened season when we only played nine games. We played them down in Washington and it was a cold, snowy day. Their kicker, Mark Moseley, beat us on a field goal, so we ended up losing 15-14. That was the year that they went to the Super Bowl with John Riggins, and it was a year after we finally made the playoffs in 1981.

We played them in the snow and it turned out to be a big game for both of us. For them, because if they won they would get home-field advantage all the way to the NFC Championship Game. We needed to win that game to go to the playoffs. I think I ended up having around 16 tackles (17 actually) and two interceptions that game. I'd compare the feeling I had in that game to a baseball player or a basketball player. They just know the pitch looks like a softball coming in or they just know they can't miss a basket. Your chemistry just feels right. You feel like you can't do anything wrong.

The next day when we were watching the game films everyone kept saying, "Man, BK, you had a hell of a game." But it was just too bad we lost that game. We really should have won it.

The biggest play I made in that game came when we were still up 14-12 in the fourth quarter. There were only a few minutes left in the game and they had a fourth-and-one near their 40-yard line. Everyone in the entire stadium knew that John Riggins was going to get the ball. That was when they had "The Hogs," and they only needed one yard.

I remember that Curtis McGriff was playing left tackle in front of me. I called a "rip" play where Curtis would come down on the inside and I'd scrape right behind him. It turned out perfect when I did that. It was just Riggins and me one-on-one. When Curtis went to the inside he took the guard off me and I just came across to the inside and scraped off his back. I had Riggins right there and I pretty much just clobbered him. As a result, they didn't get the first down.

At that point we had stopped them and we thought that we had won the game. But our offense at that time was pretty, let's just say, dormant. I'm trying to be nice here. Scott Brunner was the quarterback at the time. He came in on first down and didn't get any yards. But for some reason on second down they decided they had to pass the ball. He went back to pass and lost like 13 yards. Then it was third-and-long and he went back to pass again and got sacked again and lost another eight yards or so. So we had to punt.

They ended up getting the ball around the 50-yard line. It was a cold snowy day so the punt didn't go too far and they got great field position after the punt. We stopped them without them even getting a first down but since the punt was so bad, Moseley was able to kick a field goal to beat us.

I had a bunch of unassisted tackles in that game and two interceptions off (Joe) Theismann, so I would say that was one of my best games that I ever played in.

It's funny because Joe Theismann and I were never really big fans of one another. As everyone knew back then, Theismann had his mouth going and it went constantly. The thing I remember about Theismann was every time I'd see him during the offseason he'd ask me if I signed a new contract after every game I played against him. It seemed like I would intercept him an average of two times a season. It was just one of those things. I just had a knack for where he was throwing the ball all the time. It was a constant joke between the two of us.

But that game I actually got two picks off him. On one, I remember he was trying to hit a slant coming across the middle and I just stepped right in front of it. I thought Joe's eyes were always pretty easy to read. Especially when we had LT on the outside rushing; he was constantly looking for a receiver pretty quick. I read his eyes and was able to intercept it and make a nice return. The other one I think was what we called a flow pass when they fake one direction with all their backs and then they drag the tight end across. It was my responsibility to pick up the tight end. I was able to do it and get another interception that way. It was always great to do anything like that against Theismann.

Despite his talkativeness and my success against him, I never really had a chance to talk back at him. I never really had time to talk with anyone because I was calling all the defensive signals back then. The minute one play was over my mind immediately went to the next play. I had to quickly figure out what the down and distance was, and then look over to the sidelines to see what (Bill) Parcells or (Bill) Belichick wanted and what they were thinking. Then once I called the defense in the huddle I had to tell LT what he was doing and tell (Brad) Van Pelt what he was doing. I had a pretty full plate just trying to get the defense aligned correctly.

Unlike my buddy, Brad, I never saved any of the balls from my interceptions. I really just never got into that kind of stuff. I was there just doing my job. I never really saved any balls for myself. I do have some game balls that they painted for me and that kind of stuff, but that's really it. I got the game ball in 1981 for the playoff game against Philadelphia. Back then not that many people saved balls the way they do today. I don't even know if they would have given us a ball back then because the league was a little tighter in those days. Nowadays, everyone gets and keeps balls for things that they're supposed to be doing.

Since we lost the game to Washington, there were no game balls given. They never gave out game balls when we lost. I would have definitely gotten it. That was pretty evident. But when you lose, you don't want a game ball. I don't want a memory from a game I lost. It wasn't about the individuals, it was about the team, and that's the way we kept it back then.

Most of my career was pretty frustrating because of our suspect offense. We had one spurt in 1981 when (Ray) Perkins was calling the plays. I think Ray did a great job with our offense, building it up to be decent and respectable. But after the 1982 season, Perkins left to take the Alabama job. So that made our offense a little more dormant again.

Before that, in the '70s, we had no offense at all. I can go through a list of quarterbacks that most people have never even heard of. Guys like Jim DelGaizo, Jerry Golsteyn, Craig Morton, Randy Johnson—you name it. We went through everybody. The only running back we had back then was Ron Johnson, but he was only there until '75. We never had a running back after that. The next running back we had that was consistent was Rob Carpenter, but that wasn't until the early '80s.

For Brad, Harry (Carson), and I, that's how it was pretty much our whole career as far as never having an offense. We just accepted it.

All of the linebackers always had a tight relationship. And I attribute a lot of that to Marty Schottenheimer, who came in before the 1975 season. He coached all three of us and he's the one who developed us into quality linebackers. He kept the three of us very close. We did a lot of studying together. I think we got closer the more we realized what we had to do to become better players. And then when LT came in it only got better.

When I was playing middle in the 3-4 defense, I knew Brad and LT would never let that tight end off on me. They knew he'd just come down and crush me. They would never do it, never let it happen. So I would never have to worry about getting around the corner because I knew they'd always be pressing up the field. They were not going to let the line go downfield. It was just a confidence level that we had with each other and such a great relationship, both on the field and off. To this day, all four of us still have such a super relationship. All four of us still go on vacation together and do charity stuff together like Habitat for Humanity. We just make a point of getting together. I would say I still talk to Brad once a week, Harry twice a month, and LT maybe six times a month. We still communicate often. And our wives know each other and are good friends, too, from going on vacations together. I would never trade the relationship the four of us have for any amount of money in the world.

Now here's the story of how I ended up in New York—instead of with the hometown Cowboys. I went to a small school in California called California Lutheran in Thousand Oaks, California. At the time, that's where the Dallas Cowboys trained during the preseason. I was very fortunate to be a Kodak All-American and a Little All-American and the Cowboys were trying to keep me hush, hush. In the early '70s, ESPN was not even on anybody's map, so you could actually hide players, to a degree. Back then the scouts didn't have the ability to go to every college like they do now.

It was a situation where the Cowboys thought they could hide me and either draft me late or pick me up as a free agent. I grew up in Dallas and I was always thinking that I was going to be a Dallas Cowboy. There was no contact with the players back then during the draft. The day of the draft I was actually in the gym playing basketball. My head coach came in and told me that I had just gotten a call from the New York Giants and that they had drafted me. My jaw just dropped. I thought I was going to the Cowboys. They had told me they were going to draft me and everything like that.

At that time, I honestly didn't even know where New York was and I definitely couldn't even have named one player on the team. That's the honest truth. That was quite an experience for me.

So about a week later they called me to tell me they wanted to sit down with me regarding my contract. (Pro personnel director) Jim Trimble came out to California and picked me up at the college and we ended up going to some coffee shop where we did the contract. It was a basic deal. I think it was a $15,000 base salary, $2,500 to sign and $2,500 if I made the team. That's just the way it was back then, pretty simple and not a lot of money involved.

There were no off-season minicamps or anything like that in those days so I just flew out there for the start of the preseason. Since I really didn't know the first thing about New York, I was fortunate that I had a friend who lived in New Jersey who could pick me up at Newark Airport. He said he'd pick me up and drive me through the Lincoln Tunnel and drop me off right there because he didn't want to drive in the city. Now, I had all my bags with me because I had no idea if I was going to be there two weeks or six months if I made the team. So I had like three or four big bags with me. He dropped me off right at the exit of the tunnel and told me that I could get a cab from there. I just said, 'OK.' He took off and got to the light and saw me still standing there so he backed up and asked me if I even knew how to get a cab. I said I didn't even know what a cab looked like. That was my initiation into New York.

So after all that I couldn't wait to play Dallas, especially in Dallas. I couldn't wait to go home because all my family lived in Dallas. Those games were always special. I wanted to rub it in the Cowboys' eyes a little bit. You know, just to kind of tell them, "Hey, you should have grabbed me, you should have taken me there."

As for my entire career in New York, I'm so fortunate that I got to play with the Giants—and especially to play for a man like Wellington Mara. Just to get to be around a person like him is an honor in itself. That man made me want to be a better person. Just the way he was and the way he handled things in life and everything. He was just a marvelous man.

Obviously it turned out to be a great career for me. I was never LT or Harry Carson, but they needed a guy like me out there to control the defense. So I think I was very fortunate to come here in that situation and be that type of player and be able to play 11 years for them. The contacts and people I met out here are incredible. Heck, I moved out here from California so I obviously like it out here. Just the entire experience for me was tremendous. I can always say that I was very fortunate that I ended up being drafted by New York and that I got to play for such a great organization.

GAME RESULTS

The Giants were rolling, having won three straight contests and looking to reach the playoffs for consecutive seasons after an 18-year layoff. However, the club was rocked during the week before the Redskins game when head coach Ray Perkins announced he was going to leave the club at the end of the season to take the reins at the University of Alabama.

Needing a victory to help ensure a postseason position, New York's offense finally came through and drove on its first possession to a 28-yard touchdown connection between quarterback Scott Brunner and wide receiver Johnny Perkins. A Terry Jackson interception set up a one-yard touchdown run by Butch Woolfolk, which gave Big Blue a 14-3 lead at the break.

Through the first 30 minutes, the Giants defense was dominant, having limited the dangerous John Riggins to only 22 rushing yards and having picked off quarterback Joe Theismann four times, including Brian Kelley's pair of thefts.

After the Redskins had shaved New York's lead to 14-12, Kelley provided what appeared to be the play of the game. On a fourth-and-one from the Washington 40-yard line, Kelley, as he described, dropped Riggins for a one-yard loss with five minutes left on the clock.

But the Giants, with Brunner getting sacked twice, couldn't move the ball to kill the clock, and the Redskins were able to get themselves into Mark Moseley's kicking range. The clutch Washington kicker calmly drilled a 42-yarder with only four seconds to play for the win. The field goal was the 21st in a row for Moseley.

In the crushing defeat, Kelley led the Giants defense with 17 tackles (13 solo), two interceptions, and a deflected pass.

"I have never met or played with any football player that was more knowledgeable and more understanding about the defensive side of the game than Brian," Brad Van Pelt said. "It still amazes me that he called all the audibles and reminded LT and me every play which of us was rushing the QB when an audible would change our assignment.

"But Brian said and got it all done before the snap and still was able to play his own position to perfection. Heck, upon his retirement, Bill Parcells wanted to hire him as part of his defensive staff."

Van Pelt said none of the linebackers' success would have been possible without Kelley's assistance.

"Between Harry, LT, and I there were 24 Pro Bowl years and we all owe Brian Kelley a lot for those," he said. "There are two people I feel I owe for the success of my career, and that's Brian and Marty Schottenheimer."

Van Pelt stated how adversity made their bond stronger.

"We played 11 years together," he said. "Eleven long years that resulted in only one winning season for us. We saw it all together. But I am happy to say that because of those long years that we are like brothers today.

"He is and was the best in my book and he should have gone to all those Pro Bowls with us."

Chapter 22

BART OATES

THE YOUNG LIFE OF BART OATES

Bart Oates was never just about playing football. His days of being a scholar and an athlete started way back when he excelled on both levels at Albany High School in Albany, Georgia.

It was there that Oates learned the value and importance of putting team ahead of self.

"It was my first experience in real competitive football," he recalled. "My coach was a fair coach but a tough coach. He was building men. Championships happen and that was great, but the real motivation was to build guys who worked hard and with integrity and understood what a team was."

While Oates was catching eyes on the football field from the time he first suited up, he said he actually didn't fully grasp the concept that he belonged on the NFL level until several years into his career.

"Somewhere in the early- to mid-'90s I realized that I was okay, that I was good enough to play this game," he said. "It took a while. Even when I got into it early on, I always wondered if I was supposed to be there and if I was good enough. I knew that I had better work hard. I had to work hard because I was never sure that I was good enough to play with guys on that level. After about seven or eight years, I finally realized that I could play in the NFL. That fear of failure was probably always my biggest motivator."

It also might have been why Oates delved so deeply into another love: the law. Oates, who earned his law degree from Seton Hall University, passed the New Jersey Bar Examination in 1990 and worked as a fulltime attorney for the law firm of Ribis, Graham, and Curtin in Morristown, New Jersey, in the early '90s.

Seems the anchor of New York's offensive line could beat 'em on the field and in the court as well back in the day.

THE GAME OF MY LIFE
GIANTS AT 49ERS—JANUARY 20, 1991
BY BART OATES

I would have to say that the NFC Championship Game in San Francisco particularly sticks out in my mind. One of the reasons is that I wound up going there to play at the end of my career, and I got to see the other side and what it did to them as an organization. But, for us, it was just such a complete team game—offensively, defensively, and on special teams. It was just a game filled with us making the plays we needed to.

Jeff Hostetler came in and played so well, and we were able to move the ball offensively. The defense played well and only gave up a couple scores. The special teams, especially the field goal team and the punt coverage team, played so well. Matt Bahr made all of his kicks. If he misses one of those five kicks, we lose the game. You'd say four-out-of-five, he had a pretty good game. But nobody would remember that, now would they?

It was just what you would call an all-around complete game by all units. Anyone who ever coached in the game of football or closely followed the game would certainly appreciate watching every aspect of that game. It doesn't happen very often. There will be games when the defense dominates or the offense dominates, but very rarely that everyone makes plays.

One of the main things to come out of that game, which is something still not many people know about to this day, is that Jeff got hurt early on. He took a hit at the beginning of the game. It was really a gritty, tough performance by him. He dug in and stayed in and went on

---

Bart Oates (65) played center on both of the Giants' Super Bowl teams.
George Gojkovich, Getty Images

to make a bunch of big plays. That's one of the things I'll always remember about that game.

As a lineman, everyone knows that very seldom is the game about you. Honestly, the things I remember most from my career are the mistakes. I remember missing a block on a twist and the defensive end coming around and knocking Jeff down. Or the time that Reggie White picked me up and dumped me on top of Phil Simms for a sack. Those are the plays you remember. But from a team standpoint, and football is the ultimate team game, that game really showed what our team was all about.

And that team effort was made up of so many incredible individual performances. You had Leonard Marshall hitting Joe Montana and knocking him out of the game. Right before we hit the game-winning field goal, San Francisco ran a trap play and Erik Howard played it perfectly. That was when Roger Craig fumbled the ball. Erik Howard just split the double team between the center and left guard and he's the one who caused that fumble that LT recovered. The last sequence of plays from that game will always stand out to me.

Bob McKittrick (San Francisco's former offensive line coach) still talks about that play. When I went out there to play (after signing with the 49ers in 1994), he was still talking about it. I remember sitting down with him one day and he told me in great detail everything about that play when Craig fumbled. If they don't fumble the ball away we never get the ball back, and they just run out the clock. When Steve Young threw to Brent Jones, they got a first down and they could have just ran out the clock. But they fumbled, we got it, moved down the field, kicked a field goal, and won the game. Howard's play against the double team was huge. McKittrick taught that blocking scheme all the time. He wasn't worried about the linebacker coming across, but he wanted that offside guard, who was blocking back to the nose tackle, to make sure and be fully certain that that nose tackle was blocked. That was something he still discusses over and over and over again, and it was all because of Howard's play.

It was a great play and a great break for us. But we still had to take advantage of it. Just because it happened doesn't mean anyone gave us that winning field goal. We still had to go out there and get the ball into field goal position and kick the field goal.

Before that we had the big play on the fake punt—the play by Gary Reasons that got us a big first down. There were just all these plays we all made across the board. And we needed them because they were a terrific defensive team. As good as they were offensively, they were probably even better defensively. Joe Montana won four Super Bowls because he had a good defense on the other side of the ball. If you look, the 49ers in the Steve Young years were a better offensive team, but their defense wasn't as good then.

The mind-set coming into a game of that magnitude is that it's a do-or-die situation. You really have to think that way. It's as simple as if you win, you move on and if you lose, you go home. During the regular season you know there's always a game next week so you really don't have to play with that losing taste in your mouth too long if you drop a game. With the do-or-die mind-set, you have to take everything more seriously. Your preparation is a little more intense, you watch a little more film, and your coaches are game-planning everything a lot better.

But the funny thing is that you never really go back and look at those games again. For such an important game of such magnitude, once it was over, it was over. It wasn't like in the regular season when you dissect every little thing. We never looked at the game because we went right into preparation for the Super Bowl. We flew right to Tampa and started getting ready for Buffalo. I still have never watched the film of that game.

It was obviously a good thing that no one really remembers the play of any of our offensive linemen from that game. You usually only remember the play of offensive linemen because they did pretty poorly. Your job is to be unmemorable and uneventful. If that's how you are at the end of the game, then you've done your job. You're only noticed because you got called for a penalty or you're standing next to a teammate who just got called for a penalty.

I remember heading into the locker room after that game and there was a real sense of accomplishment because we had gotten them back after losing out there earlier in the year. We went out there and played the 49ers earlier in the season (December 3) and just got pummeled (7-3). In the two games against them—one in the regular season and another in the playoffs—we didn't even score a touchdown. But we also realized the mission was not to win that game for revenge or even the NFC Championship. That game got us to where we wanted to be: playing in the big dance. We wanted to be one of the last two teams playing. That was the goal. That's how I looked at it every year. I really never looked at it as being Super Bowl champs; I always looked at it that I wanted to be one of the last two teams playing. At that point anything can happen there.

Losing that game just killed them. They knew that they were going to beat Buffalo. If we played that San Francisco team 10 times, they would have beaten us seven or eight times. They were a better team than we were. It was close, but they were a better offense than we were, and they had a very good defense. But we won that day.

Regarding my Giants career, I was very fortunate and very blessed to be with the Giants during such a great stretch of time. I arrived in '85, which was a playoff team and a good football team. I was very fortunate to be with the Giants during some really spectacular years in the '80s and early '90s. My life has really been enriched because those are memories and experiences that no one can take from you. I have two Super Bowl rings from playing with the Giants. Some people play a long, long time and never win one. There are a lot of great players that can't say that they have a championship ring. That's what it's all about. It's the ultimate accomplishment in a team game. You can get all the individual accolades you want, but you talk to every single player and they'd trade in the Hall of Fame and all their Pro Bowl trips to Hawaii for a Super Bowl ring.

I was also fortunate to stay healthy; I never missed a game. I don't think I ever even missed a practice. At least I was healthy enough to always play. You always get hurt and you're always injured, but you just go out and play. I showed up to play. If I wanted to be remembered for anything, it would be that I showed up to work every Sunday.

Since I was a smaller guy, I always felt that I had to prepare better, play a little bit smarter, and anticipate things better. But I had pretty good quickness that allowed me to do some things that maybe some of the big, 330-pound guys weren't able to do. I wasn't the type of guy who was going to take a nose tackle and drive him five yards off the ball. As long as I prevented him from making the play, I was doing my job successfully. A lot of times I didn't look too pretty doing it, but I usually got it done. I also had good balance so I could also pass block pretty well.

I made some great associations with people in the game that I still have to this day. I still see a bunch of the guys from those teams at golf tournaments or charity dinners or even just socially.

As far as Bill (Parcells), I just loved to watch him work with players and try to motivate them. Sometimes he did it in a positive way and sometimes negatively. But he always did it with the intent of getting the best out of each player. That was his job. He obviously was good at going out and finding the best talent. Then when he had that, it was about putting together the best team with the best chemistry. Good chemistry will often overcome physical limitations. That was like our offensive line in those days. I think our biggest guy was maybe 275 pounds, but we were a good offensive line. We blocked together well, made adjustments well, and we were able to capitalize on the certain things that we did really well. Bill just had a way of putting together great team chemistry.

I was the long snapper for the first four or five years with the Giants. I remember one time in practice I was snapping to (punter) Sean Landeta and it was a pretty windy day and Sean was having trouble getting any good punts off. So Bill yelled down to him, "Hey, Sean, my mother could punt better than that." So Sean gets all fired up and takes the next punt and booms it over the returner's head. He came back to me with his little shoulder hitch and said, "I showed him, didn't I?" I just laughed and told Sean that was exactly what Bill wanted to see from him.

GAME RESULTS

The Giants snuffed out San Francisco's hopes for a three-peat as Matt Bahr's 42-yard field goal with no time remaining gave New York a 15-13 victory at Candlestick Park and sent Big Blue onto Super Bowl XXV.

As Oates described, the game-winning kick was set up by Erik Howard's heroics. He forced Roger Craig into a fumble that Lawrence Taylor recovered with only 2:36 to play. Quarterback Jeff Hostetler, who we earlier learned from Oates was playing through an injury, then took over and completed a couple clutch passes to move the team into position. First, Hostetler hooked up with Mark Bavaro for 19 yards and then Stephen Baker for 13 more.

Other Giants highlights included Leonard Marshall knocking Joe Montana silly midway through the fourth quarter and forcing the San Fran signal-caller from the game, and Gary Reasons rumbling 30 yards on a fake punt to convert a fourth-and-two later in the final period.

Oates and the offensive line allowed Hostetler enough time to throw for 176 yards and paved the way for Giants running backs Ottis Anderson, David Meggett, and Maurice Carthon to gain an additional 111 yards.

Defensively, Leonard Marshall captured Defensive Player of the Week honors for his four-tackle, two-sack, two-forced fumble contest in a game that is still remembered as one of the best conference championships in NFL history.

Chapter 23

RON JOHNSON

THE YOUNG LIFE OF RON JOHNSON

Ron Johnson, the youngest of five children, had quite a good role model to emulate growing up: his older brother, Alex.

Alex Johnson played parts of 13 seasons as an outfielder and designated hitter with the Phillies, Yankees, Cardinals, Reds, and Angels, among others. In 1970, he won the American League batting title with a .329 average.

"He was a big inspiration," Johnson said.

Johnson also credits his other brother for his development as a star athlete.

"I had a very good family," Johnson said. "Alex didn't really have the time because he was always playing baseball, but my brother Arthur would take me out and pitch to me and play catch with me and shoot baskets with me. He taught me that I needed to dribble with my left hand and things like that."

Ron Johnson, who attended Northwestern High School in Detroit, excelled in multiple sports—at least the sports he liked, and the ones they'd let him play.

"In high school, I played football, baseball, and they asked me to run track," he said. "I ran the 100-yard dash and I was never so tired in my life. I said, 'No way in heck am I ever going to do this.'"

While Johnson's track career was short-lived, he thoroughly enjoyed playing basketball.

"I went to a high school known for basketball, but they wouldn't even let me play," he explained. "They sort of portioned out the athletes in our school and tried to use athletics to get to these kids. I was told that they knew I was fine because I was playing baseball and football and that they needed a spot for somebody else.

"That's the kind of school Northwestern was back then. I played basketball every day, but they wouldn't let me play there. They basically used sports to try to get through to kids and teach them the reality of life."

It obviously worked, at least with Johnson, whose Michigan career was as impressive in the classroom as on the gridiron. But even he needed a little reassurance early on.

"I remember calling my high school coach (Van Jacobs) basically crying when I was at Michigan because there was so much competition at running back there," Johnson recalled. "He told me to shut my friggin' mouth and just go out there and play. Out of the four of us, I was lucky that I was the only one to make the traveling team my sophomore year."

Johnson said his attitude as much as anything helped him succeed on the collegiate level and beyond.

"I wasn't afraid to get into the fray and stick my head right into a 245-pounder if I had to," he said. "They just made the decision who was the best running back."

Johnson said that he played running back from day one.

"I was always a running back," he said. "The coach just put me there. And I played defensive back when I was younger."

Before he even reached high school, Johnson toiled on an all-star team of sorts.

"Growing up I played baseball and football for the Vikings," he said. "We had the best athletes in Detroit. It was the premier team in Detroit for African-Americans to play on."

Just as Johnson was always one of his team's premier athletes—whether it was on the Vikings, at Northwestern High School, at Michigan, or with the Giants.

RON JOHNSON

THE GAMES OF MY LIFE
1970 SEASON
BY RON JOHNSON

I mostly remember my first year playing in New York, which was very, very wonderful. I was drafted by Cleveland; I was their number-one draft choice. In my first couple games there, Leroy Kelly didn't play. I gained 100 yards in my first few contests. But then Leroy came back, and guess what? I didn't carry the ball any more. That was very disappointing to me.

New York needed a running back, so I got traded to the Giants. At that point, I was pretty upset. I loved Cleveland, especially being from Detroit where my parents and siblings could drive down very easily to see me play. Now they'd have to come all the way to New York. I took the trade as the Browns not wanting me, as opposed to the Giants wanting me.

I came to New York and in my first year I became the first Giant to go over 1,000 yards rushing. That was the highlight of my career. To come to New York was a lot different for me. When you're talking about speaking engagements and that type of thing, you might have gotten $100 for doing one somewhere else. In New York, I was doing commercials and getting five times as much doing the same type of stuff. Literally, most of my years here I never even touched my football salary because I was making a lot of money off the field.

That first year in New York was just absolutely magical for me.

My best games that year were obviously milestones for me. I know I topped 100 yards against the Eagles, Redskins, and Cowboys that season. But that whole year was great for me. Rushing for 1,000 yards at that time really showed the uniqueness of certain people. If you averaged four yards a carry, you're doing very well. But you have to have that extra step, that extra form to be able to turn a four-yard gain into a 10- or 12-yard gain.

I also caught a lot of passes. I'd catch the ball a lot on the A option where I'd go in the middle and fake out the outside linebacker. That was a gift play for us.

One of our best running plays was the fullback lead. Once you find the weakness in the defense you just keep running the same play until they can stop it. We'd get in the huddle and tell Fran (Tarkenton) that we

169

can run fullback lead all day. Tucker Frederickson would tell Fran that he could handle the linebacker and that he could put him on his butt every play. It was an inspiration in the huddle when guys would come back and say run this or run that; we know we can do this, we know we can do that.

It was huge to be the Giants' first 1,000-yard rusher as far as what doors it opened for me. Going back to what it means to fans and to people looking for guys to do commercials and that type of stuff, I was just totally overwhelmed by how everyone got so excited about that. I was going out speaking every day. I was talking for General Electric and basically doing everything all over the place. It was a whole new world. I'd go into a restaurant and they wouldn't charge me for anything. It was pretty much celebrity treatment.

But ultimately we wanted to make the playoffs. That was the biggest thing. It's tough to really enjoy individual numbers and accomplishments if you're not winning.

We had a really nice group of offensive linemen and they were having as much fun as I was having. They enjoyed going out there and blocking for me. They knew they had to block and that they wouldn't be getting any credit. Guess whose picture was going to be in the newspaper the next day? It was going to be Ron Johnson. But everyone appreciated that we had bonded together and that we were a successful team offensively.

I still tease Bob Tucker. He was the best friend I had with the Giants. We still see each every so often. I would kid him coming out of the huddle to make sure that he took out the defensive end. We were really what teamwork and everything that goes with it was all about. We were all on the same page together.

I still have a lot of stuff from when I played, especially from that first season. I keep it in my office, which I go into a couple times a week. All that stuff is still there. I knew that was a big part of my life back then, but thank God that I have other things that are also important to me. I feel blessed that I have too many other things going on from a positive standpoint that I don't have much time to reminisce.

When I got to New York, the running backs were Tucker Frederickson and Ernie Koy. They were two big white, fullback-type guys. Everyone assumed that if you were black, that you were fast. The Giants never really had anybody like that. So I was very, very well-received when I got to New York. I was the back that could take them to another level.

Tucker was really like a big brother to me. He helped me figure out where to go and what to do off the field. On it, he just blocked his butt off for me. He understood that from a running standpoint I was a better back than he was. But he sure could block his butt off, which he did for me.

While I thoroughly enjoyed my first year in New York, the rest of my time there was very, very disappointing. We were 9-5 that first year and missed the playoffs by only one game. Fran Tarkenton was our quarterback. He was an outstanding quarterback. But he didn't get along too well with management so they traded him. I think he was one of the best quarterbacks ever in the history of the game. For them to get rid of him was tough. Fran was very independent and they got upset with him because he would call his own plays.

We didn't have much luck in the draft during those years either. It was just so frustrating because we were at such a high level after my first season. We figured we were going to go to the playoffs the next year. But then when we started to lose, it really became no fun at all.

I'll tell you the reason why I retired. It was the last time we were negotiating contracts and they asked me why I needed all this extra money. At that time, I already worked down on Wall Street so I already had a career waiting for me. I just said to myself that this was it. Being African-American and having to answer why I needed all this money was enough for me. We were only talking about a $5,000 difference. But I just got up and walked out, and that was basically it for me. I was very frustrated.

Another misconception I had to fight was that many people thought that the only way an African-American was going to get rich in those days was by playing sports. I graduated from the business school at the University of Michigan. It was very, very important to me to keep my level of pride up. I knew I had a brain and I was going to make money with it. I didn't have to play football to be financially successful. But people assumed that the only way we'd make money was to play football, baseball, or basketball.

So I told Dean Witter, who I was working for, "I'm full-time now. Let's do it." I kept my pride after feeling very insulted by the Giants. It was time to go home.

Then I worked at Dean Witter for about four years or so. I also went into franchising, which I still do now. I opened up a Kentucky Fried Chicken in Paterson, New Jersey, in the '80s. That was my first unit. Now I have 31 of them.

My success on the football field helped open this door up for me as well. When I wanted to get involved in all of this, it was easy. I had contacted McDonald's and could have done McDonald's but I just felt that KFC was more on the up-rise as far as being able to build a business.

The best four years of my life were going to the University of Michigan. I was recruited by at least 60 schools, but just about everybody wanted me to go into Physical Education. I didn't want to go into Phys Ed.

Before that I went to Northwestern High School in Detroit, which was in an urban area. My counselors at school were just wonderful as far as giving me advice. I was president of my class and made honor roll. They kept telling me to make sure that I went somewhere where they didn't put me off as just as athlete. They made sure that if I was going to go anywhere on a scholarship that it would be to the best benefit of Ron Johnson. I just feel so blessed for all the guidance I got. My father and mother never finished school. My father told me that I'd have to handle college on my own; that he couldn't help me pay for it.

I ended up going into engineering my first year at Michigan. But it was impossible to attend all the labs I needed to for engineering and football practice so I went from an engineering degree to business school, which I really enjoyed. The next thing you know I was in the NFL.

GAME RESULTS

While Ron Johnson didn't specify any particular game from his first season in New York, he had a handful of very productive contests in 1970.

He broke out in the fourth game of the season (October 11) when he erupted for 142 yards on only 18 carries, averaging just shy of eight yards per tote. He also scored twice that day in a victory over the Eagles.

A few weeks later, he topped the century mark in back-to-back weeks for the first time in his Giants career. On November 8 against Dallas, Johnson averaged close to six yards per carry while rolling up 140 yards and a touchdown to help Big Blue top the Cowboys. The next

Sunday he led the Giants over Washington with two touchdowns among his 106 rushing yards (5.9-yard average).

He posted his fourth 100-yard game on December 6 against Buffalo, running for exactly 100 yards on 21 carries for a 4.8-yard average.

Not coincidentally, the Giants had a 4-0 record that season when Johnson reached triple figures. Perhaps coincidentally, all four contests were played at Yankee Stadium.

Chapter 24

ALEX WEBSTER

THE YOUNG LIFE OF ALEX WEBSTER

Growing up, nothing came easy for Alex Webster. He lost his father, James, when he was only nine years old. So he and his brother, who was four years younger, had to step up and help out when they were still very young.

"It was hard. My brother and I always worked," Webster said. "I used to deliver newspapers and milk early in the morning."

Fortunately for the Webster boys, their mother, Rena, had quite a strong backbone.

"My mother kept everything together," Webster said. "She kept us going. My mother worked very hard. She was a very proud lady and she worked her whole life. She died when I was in my second or third year with the Giants."

Webster also credits his junior high school football coach, Jim Gibson, for pushing him along, as well as Art Argyle, his high school coach.

"[Argyle] was another one that pushed me," he said. "He was a pusher; he was tough. He was the one that talked my mother into letting me go to college down at N.C. State."

However, coming out of college, it was no slam dunk that Webster would be able to play professionally.

"All along, I really never thought I'd reach the pro level," he said. "I was the last draft pick of the Redskins. They only had 11 picks then and I was the 11th pick. I went away to camp on a shoestring."

For what was basically a modest wage in those days.

"I signed a contract I think for $2,800 and $100 or so as a signing bonus, and I never made it," Webster recalled. "I went through the whole training camp and was one of the last to be cut."

But a fortunate run-in got his football career back on track.

"I bumped into a friend who talked me into contacting the Montreal team in the CFL," he said. "I sent an overnight telegram. In fact he was the one who turned the telegram in for me. The next morning I got a phone call and that night I was in Montreal, and the next thing you know I was a member of the Alouettes. I played the rest of the '53 season, and then I went back in 1954. We went to the Grey Cup, which is like the Super Bowl."

In a precursor to the free-agent bidding wars that go on today, the Giants basically stole Webster from Montreal.

"After the '54 season, they wouldn't give me much of a raise and the Giants offered me more money so I signed with them," he said. "The first year we played in the Polo Grounds, but then after that, I commuted from Kearny over to Yankee Stadium."

The rest, as they say, is history.

Alex "Big Red" Webster went on to a memorable playing and coaching career with New York, becoming one of the all-time most popular Giants in the process.

So, what about that famous nickname?

"I was 'Big Red' before I even got married," he laughed. "I was a real redhead. I've had that all my life."

THE GAME OF MY LIFE
GIANTS VS. BEARS—NFL CHAMPIONSHIP,
DECEMBER 30, 1956
BY ALEX WEBSTER

Of course this was so many years ago, but I'd have to say that the '56 Championship Game was my best memory. That had to be one of the

Alex Webster is fourth on the Giants' all-time rushing list with 4,638 yards. *Robert Riger, Getty Images*

highlights of my career with the Giants. It really wasn't that tough of a game, which we obviously thought it would be because it was, after all, the championship. The cold weather and what it developed into went down in history.

The game was played on a frozen field. We came out and we wore sneakers, which was something that was unheard of at that time. We had done it once before in the 1930s, when Mr. Mara got sneakers from Fordham University the day of the game. Somebody went up and opened the men's locker room and got basketball sneakers for the whole team.

I really think the sneakers had a lot to do with the lopsided score. We got off to a good start; that was the big thing. We had played them earlier in the season (November 25), and we played them to a (17-17) tie at Yankee Stadium. That was one hell of a game. So we figured we were in for a real tough one in the championship game and then to turn around and have it come so easy for us was great. Those types of games really don't happen too much, back then or today.

Looking back, I remember it was a really cold day. The wind blowing in Yankee Stadium was something else. The way the stadium is situated, the wind comes through the open end of the stands and swoops around to the closed end. So the wind swirled a lot. We probably had a little bit of an advantage there, too, because we knew what type of passes to throw into the wind and what passes to throw against the wind.

I had a pretty good game that day. I scored two touchdowns and they were both on short runs. I can barely even remember them. I never scored that many touchdowns in a game during the regular season, and then to score two in the championship game; it was a big thrill. I was really excited. I didn't even realize it or think about it until the game was over. But then, getting interviewed in the locker room by so many guys, you knew you had done something good.

More than anything, though, that game was just exciting. Plus, we made a few extra bucks for winning. I think we got around $3,600, which at that time wasn't too bad. It was an exciting game. My wife was there, too, but my kids were too small to go.

It meant a lot to win the title. It really didn't sink in until a while later. At the time, that was like the Super Bowl. The Super Bowl wasn't even around then. But that was the championship game of the world, which was quite a thrill. To win it all like that; it really didn't settle in until a few years later. People used to say that we never played in a Super Bowl, but that was the same thing, if you think about it.

These days there are so many teams involved. Back then there were only 12 of them. It wasn't that big of a deal when the players look at it today, but for us it was a big thing. We could go anywhere in the city and people recognized us. We'd go to all the famous restaurants and they'd take good care of us.

I really enjoyed playing on that '56 team. We were a very close-knit unit. I know the defense was very close. Andy Robustelli, who was one of the team captains, he really had the defense pulled together. The way he talked, he believed no one could beat them. That was his theory. Offensively, Kyle Rote and Charlie Conerly were our leaders. The defensive players stayed together. They ate together and went out and had a beer or two together. The same went for the offense. It was one close team put together in two groups.

And we had such a great coaching staff. Jim Lee Howell was an excellent head coach. On offense we had Vince Lombardi as our offensive coordinator. He was a brainchild the way he put everything together. And then on defense we had Tom Landry, who became one of the best-ever head coaches. He was a master with the defense. We had two of the best coaches in the league. Plus, Jim Lee Howell was an ex-Marine. He ran things like a Marine sergeant. He was good. He kept everybody together. It was a good all-around team and everything came together for us.

Today, the game has changed so much from when I played. The players are so much bigger, the coaches are so much more organized. They have coaches to coach the coaches. They just don't miss a trick. The coaches get all the movies and films from other games so they can prepare for every little thing. Sometimes they start looking at and scouting teams two or even three weeks before they're going to play. Everything is broken down from whether it's first-and-10 or third-and-long. And it's all charted—what they did, how they did it, what the blocking schemes were, what types of runs, etc. There are so many things involved. Teams are so well-adjusted.

These days every team would probably be prepared for sneakers and things like that. The game has advanced so much. From the uniforms to television and the way games are covered—it's all different. Plus there is so much more talent. The quarterbacks are so important with how they throw the ball. Another big thing today that no one even thought about back then is the special teams. That one kid on Chicago (Devin Hester) was a great punt returner last year. He was running them back for touchdowns all the time. That was unheard of back when I played. We had a couple of them every so often, but nothing like it is today.

I spent so many of my years with the Giants. I became a head coach later on in my life. Between playing and being the head coach, that put me on my feet pretty good. I wish I were a coach now with all the money they make. It was a great thing for me. It got me started with my family and a nice home, which we improved over time. We're still living comfortably.

My time coaching was probably the toughest five or six years I put in. It was very difficult. I loved being the offensive coordinator/backfield coach. I really enjoyed that as far as sitting down and putting everything together for a game day. Working with the players, you get very close with them. As a head coach, you really have to be on your toes. You have to set the rules. You have to be tough. But I wasn't really that tough; I let them get away with murder. I turned my back a lot of times on different things. That's just not the way a head coach is supposed to be. He's supposed to be a leader and a tough leader. He sets the rules and regulations and enforces them. You could ask any of those guys that I coached and they'd say the same thing: that I wasn't that tough. I mean, physically I could probably knock the snot out of most of them. But I wasn't tough the way I needed to be.

I still follow the guys as much as I can. I had season tickets for the longest time when we still lived up there, even after I finished coaching. I bought even more when we moved to Yankee Stadium. Then when they moved to Giants Stadium, they gave me the chance to buy four beautiful seats, which I still own. I put them in my daughter's name now. She still has a lot of tickets that she uses and also gives to friends.

I watch the Giants whenever they're on television. Down here in Florida we get mostly the Florida teams, and we get Atlanta a lot. Every once in a while we'll get the Giants, like on a Monday night. I don't really miss playing as much as I miss going to the games. I miss being around all the football people.

GAME RESULTS

Close to 57,000 fans braved the elements and packed Yankee Stadium to witness New York's third NFL championship. The Giants stole a page from their 1934 playbook when they countered the icy field conditions by donning basketball sneakers. The tactic worked then as Big Blue beat the Bears, 30-13, at the Polo Grounds, and it worked again 22 years later, as the Giants demolished Chicago by a 47-7 count to take home the 1956 title.

As Alex Webster mentioned, the Giants took the first drive of the game the distance when Mel Triplett ran it in from 17 yards out. The reeling Bears wouldn't recover, with Chicago not scoring until they already trailed, 20-0.

The Giants created that 20-0 lead on Webster's three-yard scoring run. Webster responded to Chicago's only score by taking it in from a yard out for his second touchdown and giving Big Blue a 27-7 lead. From there, it was just a matter of bleeding out the clock. Charlie Conerly tossed two late touchdowns—to Kyle Rote and Frank Gifford—to forge the final score.

Chapter 25

GARY REASONS

THE YOUNG LIFE OF GARY REASONS

We've all heard of three-sport stars in high school. Every so often you'll even hear about the extremely rare athlete who excels in four different events. Gary Reasons? Well, no one could have been all that surprised he fashioned a solid career in the National Football League after he lettered in five sports during high school.

"I was one of those kids who was always big for my size, so I was one of those guys who was always picked first in pick-up games," he said. "I was a unique kind of athlete in high school. I had a good career there."

At Crowley High School in Texas, not only was Reasons a member of the National Honor Society, but he also lettered in baseball, football, basketball, track, and golf.

"My first love was always basketball, but unfortunately I couldn't get up in the air like I needed to," he laughed.

Reasons wasn't in high school long before it became apparent that football was his sport, much to the chagrin of Reasons' baseball coach, who "went nuts" when he found out that Reasons was going to stop playing baseball his senior year so he could focus on football.

"My calling was probably football," Reasons said. "I was being recruited by major league baseball teams but that just wasn't my calling. I went on to Northwestern State and had a great football career there."

Reasons learned a lot from James Ivy, his linebackers coach in high school, and John Thompson, the defensive coordinator for his final three seasons at Northwestern State.

"James Ivy was a good fundamental coach and he taught me how to play inside linebacker," Reasons stated. "I used what I learned from him and took it into college.

"From day one in college, I was ahead of a lot of guys because I already had a background in the 3-4 defense."

That learning process continued under Thompson.

"He was a real fiery guy and he went on to have a real good college coaching career," Reasons said. "He and I hit it off really well."

So, by the time Reasons arrived in New York he had learned pretty much all he needed.

"When I stepped on the field with the Giants, I was very comfortable in that defense," he said. "The first days I was in training camp with the Giants, all the coaches will tell you that I was just a natural. They didn't have to coach me. They didn't have to tell me where to go and what to do; it just came natural to me. I made it an easy decision for them to put me on the field because they knew I was ready to play."

Reasons, who became the first player in Division I-AA history to win All-America honors in three consecutive seasons, made his mark everywhere he played.

"I wore three numbers playing football," he said. "In high school I was number 40. It was retired. In college, I wore number 34. It was retired. With the Giants I wore 55 and that's still going."

THE GAME OF MY LIFE
GIANTS AT BRONCOS—DECEMBER 10, 1989
BY GARY REASONS

We traveled out to Denver to play the Broncos in December of 1989. It was a pivotal game for us that we'd have to win to give ourselves a chance to get into the playoffs. It was a game we needed to win; there was no doubt about that. It was kind of a fun day. It was cold out there,

---

The NFL's best hit of the 1980s belonged to linebacker Gary Reasons.
Chuck Solomon, Icon Images

probably only in the 20s. It was snowing and there was snow all on the ground. It was just one of those nice, made-for-football days.

The weather was also bad back home in the East so most people were in over the weekend and a lot of folks watched that game. I actually think it was broadcast nationally. There were a lot of people that watched that game and I know that very well because a lot of them still come up to me and talk to me about it over and over again.

We were playing against John Elway and their dangerous receiving group and explosive offense. We had won our championship a couple years prior and this was the season before our next championship run. We were still a very good quality football team. After the strike year of '87 it was kind of tough for us to get back on track. That kind of hit us hard as players and as a team. I remember it took a little while for us to get our feet going, to get our feet back on the ground and get going again.

We came into that game with a 9-4 record, and it was just a game that we really needed to win. And it turned out that this was one of those games where you just know what's coming. Sometimes players get into a zone where you know what's coming and really understand how to do things well.

The first drive of the game I made three or four different tackles. I was all over the place once the game started. I had the game taped and I went back to review it and heard that John Madden made some nice colorful comments about me during the game. He said I played about as good a game at linebacker as he had ever seen. Coming from him, that's pretty poignant. It was nice to get some credit, and I felt it on the field as well.

There was a situation that came up toward the end of the third quarter that was a critical series for us. If we had any chance of winning this ballgame we had to stop Denver from scoring, and they had the ball first-and-goal from our 10-yard line. Previously on that drive, I hit Elway pretty hard a couple times and made some tackles near the sideline. I probably made like four or five tackles on that drive, yet they still drove the ball down the field on us. I made some really hard hits along the way and that's what Madden was commenting on, about how physically I was playing.

It came down to a fourth-and-goal from the one-yard line. I remember the play vividly close to 20 years later—how we were lined up defensively, and how our linebackers would fill. The play side linebacker would stuff up inside if they tried to do a dive play or a lead play with the tailback getting the ball behind the fullback, which is what we were expecting. In this case the front side linebacker, who was Lawrence Taylor, would have to step up and fill. I was the back side linebacker; I was the clean-up guy who basically had to come up over the top.

Elway's tailback at the time was Bobby Humphrey, a very highly regarded running back in the league that came out of the University of Alabama. So it was fourth-and-goal, it was snowing outside, and we needed to make this one play. I knew from their formation what the play was probably going to be and how it was going to unfold. With great anticipation and a good opportunity there, Lawrence stepped up and filled. I was on the back side; if you were looking at the defense from across the ball, I was on the right side and Lawrence was on the left. So Lawrence steps up to fill the hole and he kind of gets caught up in the traffic. Then I dive over the top of the defensive line and offensive line, fly past Elway literally in the air, and I hit Bobby Humphrey in the side of the ear hole in his helmet so hard that his ear pad got knocked out of his helmet. I stopped him two yards short of the goal line; he never even got out of his tracks. As soon as Elway handed him the ball, I hit him and it was an explosive play. Our team went wild, we stopped them and went on to win the ball game.

I knew I was going to make that play before the ball was snapped. It just kind of lined up that way. What you do defensively, you don't know exactly the play, but you can eliminate plays that they can't do based on the formation. So there was really not much of a chance of them running the ball to my side, so I was going to be the back side linebacker. That gives you the opportunity to make that kind of play. When Elway first came away from center he turned and I knew exactly what the play was so I started motioning to Lawrence and our entire defense so we all knew. They all did a good job of stopping it. But you have to get up over the top of the pile sometimes, and that's what I did.

People back east in New Jersey and all the Giants fans all remember that play. It got a lot of fanfare the next several weeks. It came to be known as the NFL's Hit of the Decade for the '80s and it's also on the NFL's top 10 greatest hits of all time. That was like a crowning moment for me to get some kudos for some good work and effort that day on the field. I played with three Cadillacs or Lamborghinis out there on the field and I was the Bronco Truck guy. When Lawrence was interviewed by

GAME OF MY LIFE NEW YORK GIANTS

CBS he made those comments and actually said something to that effect. I still kind of chuckle about that. But that's just how it was. I didn't necessarily get all the fanfare and all the ink, but that was fine with me. I just did my job.

That was a very fun game for me and a meaningful game for the team. Whenever fans talk to me about my playing career they still come up to me to this day and remember that play and that situation. Jerry Pinkus, the longtime Giants photographer, actually was there live and got a photograph of that play. He was in the back of the end zone and he caught me hitting Bobby, and he actually got a shot of the ear pad in the frame of the picture. He submitted that and I believe he won some kind of photo contest that season for an action picture. And that shot was also on a trading card that I still get sent to me all the time to get autographed. Whenever I do card shows or anything like that, there are so many people who bring that picture or that card for me to sign. If you go back and look at the 1990 media guide, I think I'm on the front. I think they put that picture on the cover. So it was just a fun memory and a fun play.

I never really reflected on my career all that much, but in addition to that Denver play, I had several other very memorable games and moments, for me and the Giants fans. Look at the 1990 NFC Championship Game. We had played a bunch of close, tough games with the 49ers leading up to that game. They were some of the best football games that you could ever imagine. They were low-scoring games and fun to watch with both clubs playing at a very high level.

In that game we played our hearts out and again, it was another low-scoring affair. There was a point late in the game where we had an opportunity to get a first down on a fourth down. We had a fake punt in our arsenal, and we never knew if we'd ever use it or call it. We had only done it once before. With me obviously being off the field when our offense had the ball, I used to run onto the field for punts on fourth down and go right by (Bill) Parcells. He'd say something to me every now and then. Well, in this situation, it was fourth down and we were around our 30- or 35-yard line and we needed seven or eight yards for the first down. He just had his arms folded and as I'm running by he said, "If it's there, run it." That's all he said to me.

So I ran on the field and checked out the situation. The way the 49ers punt return team was aligned, it was perfect for it. So perfect, in fact, and most people probably still don't know this, that the man that

188

was supposed to be right where I was going to run wasn't even out on the field. They only had 10 players on the field. Harry Sydney was their backup fullback that was supposed to be there and he didn't get out there on the field for the return. We had a fake punt that was designed to have the ball snapped right to me and I'd run right up the middle, and we'd have kind of a trap block inside. So there was a gaping hole in the middle, but with my ability we needed a gaping hole. Nonetheless it turned out to be a great (30-yard) run and it set us up for a field goal. Matt Bahr kicked it on through and we were in position to win the game, which we obviously went on to do. That was another play that a lot of fans recall fondly.

I've had other games and playoff games where I made some big plays. Earlier in my career, I had a playoff game against the 49ers (in 1984) where I had two interceptions off Joe Montana in one ballgame.

In the 1986 NFC Championship Game, the year we played the Redskins and beat them three times, I had an interception in that game as well at Giants Stadium. How fun do you think that was? That was the most electric moment that I can ever remember as a Giants player. When we played the Redskins and beat them for the third and final time that game put us into Super Bowl XXI. We were home, the fans were there, and it was a tremendous atmosphere. The Super Bowl was great and those things are fun to be involved in, but when you have a chance to play in front of all the people that have come to support you, 76 or 78 thousand strong, year after year and they get a chance to share in what you really strive for as a player, to get to the big show, to get to the big dance. To finally get there, that was by far the best atmosphere and most inspiring moment as a player because that's the game you have to win to get to the Super Bowl. Everything after that is really anticlimactic because you're expected to win the big game and we were lucky enough to win our two Super Bowls that we played in and we have the hardware to show for it. But that's what everyone strives for from the beginning of the off-season through training camp. Then when you have the opportunities to make those plays at critical times and it all comes together, that makes it all worthwhile.

I think I identified personally with a lot of what I'd call true Giants fans; people that get up and they believe and they do their job and they work hard without a lot of fanfare. That's really how I went about my career and I think I related to a lot of them. I think a lot of people looked at my career and how I went about things and the success that I had wasn't measured by how many times my picture was in the paper or in the news but just producing and making key plays at key times. There are some players who just didn't have that knack that I did. I was able to do that. My goal was never for Gary Reasons; my goal was collectively for the team to do well.

I enjoyed doing everything very much, but at the same time I was part of a great organization and a great fan base of people that lived and died with you all the same. I had a great relationship with any Giants fans that I had contact with. It's really unique for me to be able to say that.

GAME RESULTS

Gary Reasons got off to a big start in New York's basically must-win game in Denver. He made three tackles on the Broncos' first possession, which set the tone for the entire game. Reasons finished the contest with 14 tackles (11 solo) and also broke up a pass.

The Giants scored all their points in the second quarter. Ottis Anderson's three-yard run early in the second period broke the ice and David Meggett took a screen pass from Phil Simms and turned it into a 57-yard touchdown. That gave the Giants a 14-0 lead.

Reasons had three stops as the Broncos were driving for what appeared would be their first score of the game late in the third quarter. However, on third-and-goal from the one-yard line Bobby Humphrey tried to go over from the left side and was dropped by Reasons for no gain. On the next play, Reasons went up and over the line and blasted Humphrey for a one-yard loss.

Reasons' huge play protected New York's two-touchdown lead, which would prove to be essential because the Broncos were able to score early in the fourth quarter. But the Reasons-led defense held tight the rest of the game and the Giants walked out of Mile High Stadium with a much-needed and hard-earned 14-7 victory.

EPILOGUE

The Road to
Super Bowl XLVI

INDIANAPOLIS—Eli Manning never had a doubt. Not in himself and not in his teammates. When he said he believed that he belonged in the elite grouping of quarterbacks before the 2011 season, he meant it, every word of it. Then he simply went out and proved it, putting together the best season by a quarterback in the storied history of the New York Football Giants.

Don't believe us? Ask the Commissioner.

"That's a pretty elite group," Roger Goodell said after pointing out that Manning was only the fifth player ever to win two Super Bowl MVP awards. (He now joins the ranks of Terry Bradshaw, Tom Brady, Joe Montana, and Bart Starr.)

"I thought again about this business about 'elite QB,'" Giants coach Tom Coughlin said. "I think that question has come and gone."

Yes, it most certainly has. Manning capped the club's second championship in five years the same way he finished off the Patriots on February 3, 2008, in Glendale, Arizona—with the Vince Lombardi Trophy and MVP honors in hand after leading Big Blue to a late-game comeback against future Hall of Famers Bill Belichick, and Tom Brady, and their Patriots.

"For these next four or five months, we can say we're the best, we're the champs," Manning said. "That's a pretty good feeling."

Once again, Manning performed at his best when the pressure was the highest. He finished Super Bowl XLVI with 30 completions in 40 attempts, setting a Super Bowl record by connecting on his first nine passes of the game. But none of that mattered when the Giants, trailing by two points, took the ball back with a mere 3:46 to play.

Quite simply, there was no doubt. Manning had done it so many times before that the Giants weren't the least bit concerned—they knew he'd lead them to the Promised Land once again.

"With 3:46 to play, I wasn't even worried," former Giants great Michael Strahan said. "With Eli, how well he's played this year, it was actually too much time for him."

Manning quickly got to work, firing an absolute laser to Mario Manningham, who made a beautiful, athletic play to keep his feet in bounds. That play will go down as one of the greatest catches in Super Bowl history—Manning had a pea-sized opening in which to deliver the ball to the double-covered Manningham, and he did so, moving the Giants from the shadows of their own end zone to midfield in one blur of a pass.

After an incompletion, Manning connected on his final four passes of the game, pushing the Giants all the way to the Patriots 7-yard line. Once again, Manning pulled a game out in New York's final possession, and won the Super Bowl by staying cool in the most adverse of situations.

"The young man who won the MVP carried this team on his back many, many, many times," Coughlin said.

"It's been a wild day," Manning said after being named the game's most valuable player. "It's been a wild season, but we have a great, tough bunch of guys—guys that never quit and have great faith in each other. I'm just proud of our team and the way we've dealt with everything all season and came out strong."

Strong was certainly the most accurate word to describe the Giants desire to make Manning a Giant in the 2004 NFL draft. So much of the credit goes to former GM Ernie Accorsi, who absolutely fell in love with Manning's calm, cool demeanor—a critical characteristic which has helped him tremendously in the bright spotlight of New York. Manning is unwavering, keeping a level head at all times, on the field and off. And the Giants have two Super Bowl titles to show as a result.

"When I think of what we went through to try to get him back in 2004 and how he almost didn't become a Giant, I'm happy it worked out the way it did," Giants owner John Mara said. "Ernie Accorsi and Tom [Coughlin] and [current GM] Jerry Reese had a conviction about him and that conviction has paid off."

Boy, has it ever.

"I felt like he took the entire team under his wing, he lifted everyone around him," Mara continued. "I remember Ernie's scouting report from when Eli was at Ole Miss: He said he doesn't have the best talent around him, but he makes everybody better. Man, there are not too many guys like that on the planet."

Perhaps what's most impressive is how much better Manning played during almost all of this season than he had in any previous campaign. His teammates noticed how he showed up for the season raring to go and as ready as he's ever been. He also seemed to benefit from the tutelage of QBs coach Mike Sullivan, who helped challenge Manning mentally and physically.

"He's awesome," Giants linebacker Michael Boley said. "Just to go from where he was last year to this year is impressive. It just shows the hard work he put in throughout the offseason, getting his body and mind right. He's battled a lot of adversity this year and I take my hat off to him."

Fellow defender Linval Joseph finished his second campaign with the Giants and was similarly blown away by how much progress Manning made between the 2010 and 2011 seasons.

"This year from last year, he really grew up," the defensive tackle stated. "This year, he's been a full leader. I've watched him. He leads his team. There are so many things he did this year that he didn't do last year and it helped us out so much in the long run. He threw for almost 5,000 yards. He talked to the receivers and got them all on the same page. He had everybody working together and it showed [in the Super Bowl] and all season."

Perhaps Manning's greatest contributions came when no one could see. His tireless time spent talking to, and watching film with, the Giants receivers resulted in the Giants boasting one of the league's most feared passing attacks. Mario Manningham and Victor Cruz, especially, have benefitted from Manning's leadership.

When most Giants were waiting out the lockout all around the country, it was Eli Manning holding workouts at Hoboken High School in northern New Jersey for a handful of receivers. To say Manning goes above and beyond the call of duty would be a gross understatement.

But with all that said, the 2011 season was hardly a cakewalk and a championship coronation. Manning and the offense struggled out of the gate. One year after throwing 25 interceptions to 31 touchdowns, Manning and the Giants staff knew a huge reduction in turnovers would be required for the Giants to actually live their Super Bowl dreams. What you found was a signal-caller showing much more patience with his receivers, a QB that didn't force the ball into tight spots, a tough leader that would take the sack instead of tossing the pigskin into harm's way.

The results were noticeable: only 16 INTs to 29 TDs, and a club single-season record 4,933 yards. Manning also clearly earned the billing as one of the game's top comeback artists with an NFL-record 15 fourth-quarter TD passes, and also one of the game's most successful passers on third down.

While it seems like light-years away from the end of a season that ended in championship fashion, opening day for the Giants was ugly: they lost for the first of two times to the undermanned Redskins. Things continued to be a little rocky in Week Two, but Manning, as he proved he could do all season long, rallied the troops with a pair of TD passes in a home-opening win over the Rams.

Week Three was when the NFL world started to notice the Giants as potential players. They went into Philadelphia and handily knocked off the Eagles by a 29-16 count. All Manning did that afternoon was throw four touchdowns passes with nary an INT and compile a season-high 145.7 QB rating.

Another comeback victory in Arizona had the Giants sitting pretty with a 3-1 mark at the quarter pole. But all those smiles were turned upside down the next week during one of the club's worst efforts of the season. Manning was intercepted three times and sacked three more during a simply awful 36-25 loss at MetLife Stadium to the Seahawks, of all teams.

New York quickly and strongly bounced back, ripping off three straight wins to reach midseason with a 6-2 mark and a two-game lead in the NFC East. Big Blue won consecutive home contests with Buffalo and Miami before heading up to New England. No surprise at all there that Manning, via his two TD passes, was able to pull it out at the end as the Giants came from behind and knocked off the Pats, 24-20, handing Tom Brady his first home loss in an amazing 31 games.

"I'm just happy he [Tom Brady] left us enough time. Guys just hung tough and found a way to win," Manning said after connecting with Jake Ballard for the game-winning points with only 15 seconds to play.

"They just made some pretty good plays there at the end to win it," Brady said, in more than a little bit of foreshadowing.

But then the unthinkable happened. The Giants went from on top of the world—or the division, at least—to 6-6 seemingly in the blink of an eye. New York lost four consecutive games, during which Manning threw for 8 TDs and 5 INTs. Close losses in San Francisco and against Green Bay sandwiched an awful effort against the Eagles at MetLife Stadium and a blowout defeat in New Orleans.

A Sunday night trip to Dallas on December 11, 2011, was perhaps Manning's best masterpiece of the season. He led the Giants back from a 12-point deficit with less than four minutes to play, bringing the Giants back into a tie at the top with the Cowboys.

The heartbreaking home loss to Washington followed, but, to a man, the Giants focused on the fact that they still controlled their own destiny and would clinch a playoff berth with two victories in their final two games.

They wouldn't lose again.

The Eli Manning/Victor Cruz 99-yard TD was the biggest play of the season, and it allowed the Giants to knock off their in-stadium rivals, the Jets, on Christmas Eve. That led to a win-and-in battle for the NFC East title with Dallas. There would be no Wild Card berth for the loser; just a ticket straight home. The Giants won that one easily, as Manning threw for 3 TDs and no INTs and the Giants were NFC East Champs despite a 9-7 record.

Another 3-TD, no-INT game for Manning led to another easy win, this one over Atlanta at MetLife Stadium by a 24-2 count in the opening round of the playoffs. Another three touchdown passes from Manning led the Giants over the top-seeded Packers in Green Bay by a 37-20 count.

They had gained revenge on the Packers for a regular season loss and would now get the same opportunity in San Francisco against one of the game's most feared defenses in the NFC Championship Game. Manning showed how physically tough he was in this contest, taking hit after hit while he was sacked 6 times and pressured a total of 20 times. But it was his refusal to make a mistake that allowed the Giants to get into overtime, where they would win it on a huge special teams play by rookie LB Jacquian Williams.

The rest, as they say, is history. The Coughlin/Manning combo knocked off the Belichick/Brady duo once again and the Giants had captured their fourth Super Bowl title, the only franchise to win a Super Bowl championship in each of four consecutive decades. They also became the first ever 9-win team to win it all.

Former Giants WR Amani Toomer was so happy to see Manning once again succeed at the highest level.

"Eli's unbelievable," Toomer said. "He really understands what he's doing. He's a pleasure to watch. I know he had some adversity he needed to get through. They gave him all that money and it hasn't changed him even a little bit. I'm so happy for him and proud of him."

As always, Manning deflected praise after winning the MVP honors.

"It just feels great," he said. "It was a great game with two great teams. We played to the very end. It was just a great effort on both sides. There were some big plays being made.

"I'm just happy for the guys. I'm happy for everyone in that organization, Coach Coughlin, all of my coaches, all of the players getting a chance to win the Super Bowl. Some of these guys are getting their first one. I feel great for them. I feel great for everybody."

Manning and Coughlin will forever be joined in history. Heck, at this rate they just might end up together in Canton as well, down the road. Simply put, Coughlin couldn't ask for more from his offensive captain and two-time Super Bowl MVP quarterback.

"Eli epitomizes everything I believe in as a player," he said. "There's a strong bond there."

Rookie CB Prince Amukamara was very impressed with Manning all throughout this championship season.

"Eli is amazing," Amukamara said. "Everyone gave him crap early in the year for saying that he's one of the best and should be up there with Brady and those guys. I think he definitely proved himself this whole season. Eli should definitely be mentioned with being the best in this game."